YOUNG TEENAGE READING HABITS:

a study of the Bookmaster scheme

Jean Bird

British National Bibliography Research Report 9

Abstract

During school summer holidays, Westminster Children's Libraries operate graded reading schemes open to all comers. This report is an account of a survey during summer 1981 of 312 scheme users and a further 168 scheme non-users, aged between 11 and 18. Various sources of information were utilized, including formal questionnaires, informal tape-recorded interviews and book reviews written by the scheme users. Among the variables considered there were few significant differences between scheme users and non-users. It was concluded that the schemes do persuade many children to read more books more thoroughly and to enjoy the experience of reading more, but not necessarily to read different kinds of books. Further information is needed about public library use by the over-14s. In view of the current interest in the under-achievement of girls, it seems that the self-imposed demarcation between "boy's" and "girl's" reading warrants further attention.

BNB Reseach Fund Reports are published by the British Library

ISBN 0 7123 3007 0
ISSN 0263-1709

The opinions expressed in this report are those of the author and not necessarily those of the British Library or the British National Bibliography Research Fund.

Typeset by The Palantype Organisation Limited, 4 North Mews, London WC1N 2JP and printed in Great Britain by DND Business Services, Tadcaster, North Yorkshire

Contents

List of figures

List of tables

Foreword

There is no doubt that Westminster's summer reading schemes for children and young people — Bookworm, Bookwizard and Bookmaster — are highly desirable in themselves. The staff in the children's libraries now have several years' experience of organizing such schemes, and it is clear that they have been responsible for developing and widening the reading interests of thousands of Westminster youngsters.

By now it should be unnecessary to mention that while some parts of Westminster are populated by the relatively affluent, there are other parts in which the poorest socio-economic conditions prevail. These extremes, together with the multi-racial nature of the population in most areas of the City, mean that Westminster (whatever its name implies) is subject to the problems and challenges which face any of the other boroughs or cities more frequently quoted as suffering from urban and inner-city stress. It is against this background of contrasts that the children's librarians work; the enthusiasm with which young people, parents and teachers support the summer reading schemes is but one example of the success of the staff in seeking to relate their services to local community needs.

As the reading schemes developed over the years, however, staff became increasingly aware of the problems of one particular group, aged approximately 11 to 18. While the Bookmaster scheme had been worthwhile in promoting and widening fiction reading in this age group, lack of knowledge about their book preferences and the relevance of the library to their needs had been brought home.

Is the right sort of reading material available in the libraries? Indeed, is it available at all? And if it is available, how should it be presented and promoted? Such questions are of vital relevance not only to librarians, but to every section of the book trade from the author onwards. It was logical, therefore, to embark upon an investigation in this field and to use the Bookmaster scheme as a basis. This report, which hopefully will be found fascinating and of genuine value to the book world, is the result of that investigation.

It gives me great pleasure to acknowledge the interest taken by the British National Bibliography Research Fund, without whose financial support the work would not have been possible. We were most fortunate to secure the services of Jean Bird, to whom we owe gratitude for the exemplary and painstaking manner in which she has carried out the research and presented the results. In addition, I acknowledge the skillful work carried out by Erika Winstone, her research assistant on the project. Thanks are also due to Lorna Roberts and her team of staff, who fully participated at the same time as organizing the usual 'nuts and bolts' of the three reading schemes in an even busier summer period than in previous years, to the University of London for access to their computer, and Alina Vickery for her unfailing kindness and assistance in programming. Finally, we are grateful to the staff of the British Library Research and Development Department, in particular to Irene Muir, who has always been available for help and advice.

MELVYN BARNES
City Librarian, Westminster

1 Introduction

During the summer of 1981, a survey was carried out of young people aged between 11 and 18, using Westminster City Children's Libraries. This report forms an account of this survey and discussion of its findings.

1.1 Westminster Junior Libraries' summer reading schemes

During the school holidays, Westminster's eight main junior libraries operate a graded series of reading schemes (see Appendix 1), open to all children under 18. These were started in 1975, and by 1981, were attracting nearly 1,500 children. Three schemes are currently in operation: Bookworm, which requires that five books be read; Bookwizard, which requires that five books be read plus one review written; and Bookmaster, which requires that four books be read and all reviewed. These are minimum requirements and some children read many more than is necessary to complete the scheme. Various inducements and rewards, such as badges, certificates, name displays in the branches, and presentation ceremonies form part of the scheme, plus, of course, the pleasures of reading good books and talking to the librarians. The library staff talk to every child about every book read, and it is not surprising that operating the schemes requires a considerable amount of paperwork and careful organization.

In 1980, the opportunity was taken to extend unobtrusively the usual registration form of one group of children — the Bookmasters. This was the hardest scheme and only children aged 11 or over are eligible. These children form a minority of scheme users and it was felt that more could be known about these older children using the schemes. Expanding the registration forms with a few more questions proved to be a straightforward and simple exercise and demonstrated very clearly that Westminster's junior users had got so used to filling in forms and answering questions for the librarians, that a survey on a much larger scale would not be unduly daunting to them.

It was therefore decided to carry out as comprehensive a survey as possible, of children aged 11 and over, using the junior libraries during the summer of 1981.

1.2 The research project

A proposal was submitted to the British Library Research and Development Department, for a brief three-month project, to commence in July 1981. It was funded by the British National Bibliography (BNB) Research and Development Fund, to employ one full-time research worker and one temporary library assistant to be seconded to the project. In practice, a part-time research worker was appointed and the work was carried out over a five-month period between June and October 1981.

1.2.1 Aims

Although Westminster's initial interest was in the children using their reading schemes, they were also interested in the 11+ age group as a whole, and the project aims were formally defined as:

(a) to explore book preferences of young people aged 11 to 18, who have either enrolled in a Westminster City Children's Libraries' reading scheme, or who use the libraries over the same period without enrolling in any scheme;

(b) to collect basic data on the use, attraction and observable effects of the reading schemes;

(c) to explore certain aspects of library use among young people in this age group.

The survey was confined to junior library users, and all interviewing was carried out in the libraries.

1.2.2 Methods

Formal questionnaire interviewing and informal tape-recorded interviewing were the main methods of data collection used, but existing sources of information were also occasionally utilized, e.g. reviews written by the children.

The interviewing methods were:

(a) questionnaire administered to children, aged 11-18, who were not enrolled in any reading scheme, using eight branches throughout one week;

(b) the same questionnaire administered to children, aged 11-18, enrolled in a reading scheme in the same eight libraries. The schemes started on 13 July and ended on 4 September, and questionnaires were administered throughout this period. These children were also given a further shorter questionnaire relating solely to scheme use;

2

(c) a small sub-sample of scheme users were selected to provide case studies. These children were interviewed on tape using a prepared interview schedule and a dossier was built up on each child, consisting of librarian's comments, the taped interviews, questionnaires (completed before the child was selected for further interview), and reviews.

(For more detailed information about methodology and questionnaires used, see Appendix 2.)

The total number of children in the sample was 480, of whom 312 were scheme users, 168 non-scheme users. Twenty children were further interviewed on tape; ten case studies are reproduced in this report.

The quantitative results were analysed on a Commodore Pet Computer at Central Information Services, Senate House, University of London.

1.2.3 Scope

It is hoped that the information and ideas put forward in this report will provide useful insights for all those interested in the reading habits of the 11+ age group, and that it will help to provide some guidance for those concerned with producing, promoting or providing books for young urban teenagers.

2 Eleven-plus junior library users

2.1 Age

The great majority of the sample were aged between 11 and 14.

Figure 2.1 Age of junior public library users over 11: whole sample

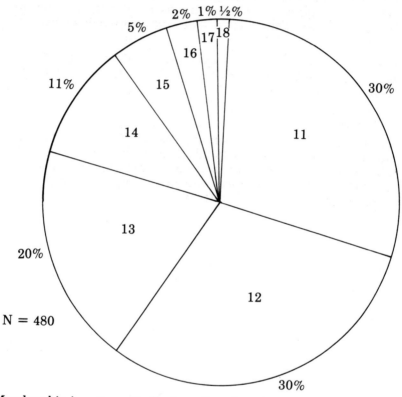

Membership is automatically transferred to the adult library at 14, although members may, and do, continue to use the junior library.

It is interesting to speculate on what happens to the over-14s. Do they simply stop using the library as influence of school in particular decreases; do they use the adult library; do they stop using libraries after using the adult library or without ever trying it?

Interest in reading is said to peak around the age of 11[1]. Does this mean that library use will always decrease with age throughout teenage years? Brenda Jones[2] found in a survey of 602 school-children aged between 11 and 14, that while use decreased with age, ability band was more important than age, so that 14-year-olds in the highest ability band were *more* likely to be using the public library at 14, than at 11. She also found that children in all ability bands used the public library primarily for 'story' books, implying that higher ability children were not using public libraries primarily for school work. Does this mean that the fiction in junior public libraries designed for their older readers is most suited to higher ability children? What is certain is that over-14s are heavily under-represented among summer junior library users.

2.1.1 Age and scheme use

Westminster's summer reading schemes appear to be more attrac-tive to young readers in the age group 11-14, which would corres-pond with the suggested peak in reading interest at age 11 (see Table 2.1).

Table 2.1   Age of scheme users/non-users over 11

Age	Scheme users %	Scheme non-users %	Total sample %
11	35	23.25	30
12	32	27.25	30
13	19	20.25	20
14-18	14	29.25	19.5
	N = 312	N = 168	N = 480

2.2   Sex

Just under two-thirds of the sample were girls, just over one-third boys (see Table 2.2).

2.2.1 Sex and scheme use

More girls were attracted to the schemes than boys (see Table 2.2).

5

Table 2.2 Sex: whole sample, scheme users/non-users

	Girls %	Boys %	
Total sample	64	36	N = 480
Scheme users	68	32	N = 312
Non-users	58	42	N = 168
	N = 307	N = 168	

2.3 Sex and age

The boys were rather more likely to be younger than the girls (see Table 2.3).

Table 2.3 Age of boys and girls: whole sample

Age	Boys %	Girls %	Total sample %
11	31	29	30
12	34	28	30
13	17	21	20
14-18	18	22	19.5
	N = 168	N = 307	N = 480

Numerically, the largest groups of library users over 11 were: 11-year-old girls (18%); 12-year-old girls (18%); 13-year-old girls (13%); 12-year-old boys (12%); and 11-year-old boys (11%).

These five groups account for 70% of users.

2.3.1 Sex, age and scheme use

Bearing in mind that the girls were slightly more likely to be older than the boys, and that the schemes were more attractive to the girls, one would expect scheme users to be slightly older than non-users. In fact the reverse is true (see Table 2.1), indicating that it is the younger girls in particular who are most attracted to the schemes.

2.4 Ethnic background

The Department of Education and Science (DES) has clearly stated the grounds for public libraries sustaining interest in the ethnic background of library users:

'The cultural, information and educational needs of members of ethnic minority groups are not necessarily distinct from those of the rest of the community. But they may be, some want special materials in order to maintain their cultural identity. Some want materials for learning English as a second language. Furthermore ... Library Authorities in all parts of the country should recognize and promote a positive awareness of the multi-cultural nature in our society.'[3]

There is no doubt that London is highly multi-cultural, and Westminster is no exception to this.

In the sample, 46% of the children were judged to belong to a specified minority ethnic group, although definition of a minority ethnic group was fairly arbitrary. For example, Irish children were not identified as a separate ethnic group although there are many Irish children in London. For this reason, the other 54% of the children are referred to as 'others' (see Table 2.4).

It may be noted that the Inner London Education Authority (ILEA)[4] was slightly surprised at the proportion of European children, who accounted for over 50% of pupils for whom English was not a first language, in Division Two (Westminster and Camden). Spanish children were the largest group among such pupils, with the other main groups being Greek, Chinese, Italian, Portuguese, Bengali and Arabic children, in numerical order.

There is no doubt that Westminster's junior libraries are serving a multi-ethnic population, as they are quite fully aware.

2.4.1 Ethnic background and scheme use

Non-users were slightly more likely to be members of ethnic minority groups. European children in particular were under-represented. (Spanish children were the predominant group among Westminster's 'European' users, but in comparison with ILEA's

Table 2.4   Percentage of specified ethnic minority groups:
whole sample, scheme users/non-users

Ethnic minority group	Scheme users %	Non-users %	Total sample %
West Indian	14	17	15
Indian	12.5	11	12
European	6	12	8
Arabic	3.5	4	4
Chinese/Malay	4	6	5
African	1	2	1
Others	59	48	55
	N = 312	N = 168	N = 480

figures, Spanish and Portuguese children are under-represented among library users generally. ILEA found that a high proportion of Greek, Spanish, Portuguese and Arabic children were to be found in Division Two, which includes Camden.)

2.5   Languages spoken

It may be that the obligation to reflect pluralism and to help children to whom English is not a first language to enjoy and benefit from reading in English, is greater than the obligation to provide books for children in mother-tongue languages — not least of all because of the extraordinary diversity of mother-tongue languages to be found in London.

In 1978, when ILEA[5] obtained statistics on mother-tongue languages of pupils, it analysed the results using 38 language categories. Some of these were catch-all headings such as 'other European', 'other Middle-East', 'other West Indian', and so on, and they still required a final 'other' category at the end of the list!

Children were asked what spoken language was 'preferred' at home.

A small number of children — usually Indian or Greek — said that they spoke English to siblings but mother-tongue to parents. Most children had no difficulty — or showed any hesitation — in answering this question.

Seventy percent of the sample said English was the only language spoken at home, a further 14% said it was the preferred language at home, and another 12% stated that a language other than English was preferred at home. The remaining 4% said that they did not speak English at home at all. ILEA found in Division Two that 15% of the total school roll were pupils for whom English was not a first language. This would indicate that such children are not under-represented among library users, although ILEA points out that these children were all identified by their teachers, who may well have missed children who spoke English well but nevertheless spoke a different language at home.

2.5.1 Languages spoken and scheme use

Scheme users were somewhat more likely to cite English as their only language (70% scheme users: 62% non-scheme users). They were also less likely to say that they did not speak English at home (2% scheme users: 8% non-scheme users).

2.6 Languages read

Not all the children who regard English as their second language have difficulties in reading English. ILEA estimated that just over a quarter of such children required further tuition in English, at secondary school age, in Division Two. The proportion is much higher for primary school age children.

Two percent of the sample gave a non-English language as preferred reading language, mainly Spanish, but some Arabic. Another 11% cited a language other than English as one that they read in. (Languages learnt as part of a school curriculum were rigorously excluded.) Several of these children mentioned that they would read more in these languages if they could find any books in them. Spanish and Arabic were again in evidence, also several Indian languages.

2.6.1 Languages read and scheme use

Scheme users were slightly less likely to cite a language other than

English as being preferred and less likely to cite any reading language other than English (9% scheme users: 14% non-users) although proportions in both groups are small. It would seem that the library users form a diverse group ethnically but that very few children in the age group who are not happy reading in English, use the library.

2.7 Length of residence

Westminster is said to have a very transient population[6]. A total of 97% of the sample of library users had lived in London for either over five years (88%) or between one and five years (9%) suggesting that the libraries do not attract many children new to London in this age group (see Table 2.5).

2.7.1 Length of residence and scheme use

Scheme users were slightly more likely to be longer term residents than non-users, but the differences are not significant.

Table 2.5   Length of residence: whole sample, scheme users/non-users

Length of residence	Scheme users %	Non-users %	Whole sample %
Over 5 years	89.5	85	88
1-5 years	8	11	9
Under 1 year	2.5	4	3
	N = 312	N = 163	N = 480

2.8 Distance from library

Ninety-four percent of the sample lived in Westminster, and virtually all these children lived within easy walking distance of their branch. Of the remaining 6% (27 children), most of them lived in adjoining boroughs, also quite close to the branch used. Eighteen of these children were Westminster junior library members.

10

2.8.1 Distance from library and scheme use

The schemes did not appear to attract many more children from outside Westminster than would be expected, although they did attract five children who were members of other public library authorities, as opposed to the non-scheme library user who was a member of another library authority. The conclusion must be that the library's clientele is overwhelmingly drawn from children living nearby, even in this older age group and despite the attraction of a scheme that is unique to Westminster.

It may also be noted that Brenda Jones[7] found in her sample of 11-14 year olds that the most often cited reason given for non-use of public libraries was 'public library too far away'.

2.9 Library membership/use

Overwhelmingly, the children in the sample were members of Westminster libraries (91% junior members, 8.5% adult members). Also, three-quarters of the sample were regular library users.

It is interesting to note that a majority of the sample said that neither of their parents were members of any public library.

Twenty-nine percent of the children came with friends, 11% with

Table 2.6 Library membership, regular library use and parental membership: scheme users/non-users

	Scheme users %	Non-users %
Westminster library member	94	85
Regular library user	78	66
Non regular user	22	34
Parents member of a public library	46	39
Parents not public library members	54	61
	N = 312	N = 163

11

parents, 38% on their own and a further 25% with other members of their family (usually siblings).

2.9.1 Library membership/use and scheme use

Scheme users were rather more likely to be library members than non-scheme users, and were also more likely to be regular library users. They were also somewhat more likely to have parents who were public library members (see Table 2.6).

It may be noted that just over 10% of the children said they came to meet friends or just for something to do, and not surprisingly, non-scheme users were more likely to cite this as a reason for their visit, than scheme users.

3   Library users: opinions and ideas

It is notoriously difficult to elicit opinions and ideas from library users, many of whom have very few strong opinions about public libraries, other than a vague feeling that they must be a 'good thing'. Although it was felt that children might be less inhibited about this than adults, it should be remembered that the library staff themselves distributed and collected most of the questionnaire, and had to read through the questionnaire to check for completeness.

Therefore only three general questions were asked about libraries but they did all deliberately encourage the children to verbalize any problems, or ideas for improvements, that they may have had, rather than discuss, or express, their satisfaction with the existing service. (In fact the question asking the children to indicate any ideas they had for improving the library was specifically retained, following piloting, at the request of the branch librarians who were interested in hearing what the children had to say about this.) Thus, the following comments should be interpreted within this context.

The first of these questions was 'What kind of books would you like us to have more of?'. The second question stated 'Other library users have mentioned problems in finding good books in this library. Tell us if you agree or disagree with the following things'. The third question was totally open-ended and asked respondents to write down 'any ideas you have which could make the library better for you'.

3.1   Responses to suggested problems of library use

These five statements were suggested to the children:
- (a) too many books are too hard to read;
- (b) too many books are too long;
- (c) too many books are all words;
- (d) it's difficult to choose a book from all the books on the shelves;
- (e) I do not understand how all the books are arranged.

Almost two-thirds of the sample agreed that it was difficult to choose a book, over one-third agreed that too many books were all words (not enough illustrations) and just under one-third agreed

Table 3.1   Percentage agreeing with suggested problems of library use: whole sample, boys/girls, scheme users/non-users

Statements	Total sample %	Girls %	Boys %	Scheme users %	Non-users %
Too many books are too hard	19	17	22	19	19
Too many books are too long	32	32	32	30	36
Too many books are all words	41	38	46	39	46
It is difficult to choose a book from all those on the shelves	65	67	64	66	64
I do not understand how all the books are arranged	30	27	34	23	34

N=48   N=307   N=168   N=312   N=168

that too many books were too long. The same proportion agreed that they did not understand the arrangement. There was least agreement with the statement that too many books are too hard.

It may be noted that Fenwick[8] found that length of book and proportion of illustration was more significant than a child's reading ability, and that the DES[10] found 'over half the sample experienced difficulty in locating suitable books to read in a library'.

3.1.1 Responses and scheme users

Non-scheme users were slightly more likely to agree that too many books were too long, were all words, and that they did not understand the arrangement (see Table 3.1).

3.1.2 Responses and age/sex

Differences between age groups were greater than differences

14

between the sexes (see Tables 3.1 and 3.2). It was interesting to note that at least a third of all age groups agreed that too many books were all words, bearing in mind that this was a sample of children who were almost certainly more avid and able readers than one would find in a sample drawn from these age groups generally.

Table 3.2 *Percentage agreeing with suggested problems of library use: age groups*

Statement	Age groups					Whole sample
	11	*12*	*13*	*14*	*15+*	
Books too hard	22	21	13	17	12	19
Books too long	30	37	34	29	17	32
Books all words	51	38	36	35	42	41
Difficult to choose	69	70	64	64	50	65
I do not understand arrangement	33	29	32	27	25	30

N=141 N=143 N=93 N=54 N=39

3.2 Ideas about how to make the library better

This question (Question 11 on the questionnaire) was not 'compulsory'. If the children could not think of anything to say, or did not want to reply, they were not prompted in any way.

Half the children did choose to reply to this (240 children), of whom 18 said it was fine as it was, sometimes very enthusiastically:
    'This library is in tip-top shape.'
The other children made suggestions that were grouped into four main categories: guidance/classification; activities; more resources; library procedures/organization.

3.2.1 *Guidance/classification*

Although this category is rather a pot-pourri, covering subject classification, fiction categorization, shelf guidance, catalogues, book lists and user instruction, they form a coherent group because of the focus of the children's interest. The children saw all these things in terms of devices to help themselves find the books they wanted — very little mention was made of librarians as intermediaries in this process. The suggestions were all designed to make it easier for them to choose or find the books they wanted, ultimately by themselves.

In any survey of library users, some people will spontaneously invent classification, cataloguing, user instruction, shelf guides, and so on, sometimes to the despair of librarians who may have been trying hard actively to promote the existence of such facilities.

The children in this sample were well up to this task, and many of the comments were in fact quite sophisticated — machinery and technology does not alarm modern youngsters. In total, a third of the suggestions about improving the library fell into this category, which made it the largest single category, and although it can be very frustrating for librarians to read suggested 'improvements' when they know they already exist, it is as well to remember that to the user, 'reality' is what they see, not what is. It seems that the need for user education is as great as ever, and exists at earlier and earlier ages. The Southgate Report[9] looking at seven to nine year olds said:

'One of the most important findings of this research is that children in this age group require more specific training in the use of books'.

It could be said of this research that one significant finding is that young users seem also to want more practical guides and guidance to their libraries.

'I wish there was a little table where you can get advice.'
'More books on show to give us an idea of what books you have.'
'Our own cataloguing system whereby we could look up ourself to help us understand the arrangement.'
'A piece of paper in each book telling about it.'
'A title catalogue.'
'Alphabetical guide to books.'
'To have codes on the story books so you know what they are.'
'Name the shelves — animals, sports ....'
'The idea is that the mysterious books should go on one shelf, the adventures on another — like this it would be easier to find books.'
'More signs to help you find particular sorts of books.'
'Clearer ways to find books like a marker to show the beginning or end of a section.'
'I find it hard to understand how to use the library. I think you

should write a paper to tell how to use the library.'
'Have a different subject of books each week, in a box.'
'A big chart with all the books about animals and a number beside it — you look at it and the number tells you where the book is.'
'Have this drawer with letters like A-C and have all the books that begin with it there, and suppose you want to find out about Cats, look under 'C' and then you find the card and have to look at the number, then go to the place where the number is.'
'Suggested good books to hand out.'
'Put special topic books in one area.'
'Books for older people should be separate from those for younger people.'
'Sections for different ages.'
'Special section on books for teenagers.'
'It could be split into fiction books and non-fiction books and maybe put in alphabetical order.'
'Exhibitions are a bit babyish. Maybe there could sometimes be an exhibition featuring a particular writer.'
'Have an author month where you have a special display about one author showing all their work.'

3.2.2 Activities

Just over a sixth of the replies to this question mentioned activities of various sorts. Users' expectations tend to be structured by their library experience, and this was apparent in these replies, nearly all of which were centred around extending existing activities.

Several suggestions related to extending the reading schemes or other ways of extending reading and interest in books.
'A reading group for children at weekends and holidays.'
'A book swap club.'
'Discussion groups — library competitions — creative writing.'
'Find out if I am good at writing stories by asking me to write stories for you.'
'Have Bookworm and things not just in the holidays because most holidays I am away.'
'More schemes like Bookmaster.'
Other suggestions included: 'librarian-for-a-day' schemes; decorating the libraries with posters; playing board games; special library projects; and simply 'having more to do than just read'.
'An evening club to decorate the library with posters.'
'Put your name on a list and help in the library stamping books

like we do at school.'
'Should have special library projects every summer — asking questions, having tests.'
'I would like to see the library find out about libraries in other countries.'
'Play games like Monopoly in the holiday.'
'To have more things to do than just working or reading.'

There is strong evidence that many children prefer to do their actual reading at home, rather than at school or in a library (see Table 3.3), and educationalists have long recognized the value of 'extension' activities such as language games in developing necessary skills for effective reading. It could be that there is a close relationship between promoting 'activities' in junior libraries and promoting a lifetime habit of reading.

Table 3.3   Preferred place of reading for children aged 11*

Preferred place of reading	Children aged 11 %
Home — bed/bedroom	54
Home — otherwise	14.5
Outdoors	3
School	7
A library — school or public	4
Unspecified but peace and quiet/alone/ undisturbed	17.5

N = 1,161

3.2.3 More resources

Nearly 40% of the children wanted 'more' of various things, although the suggestions were indeed many and various, with no one single item predominating. The largest single category of answers was in terms of more books, often left just at that, but occasionally specified further — more ghost, adventure, mysteries

* Source: DES, 1981. *Language performance in schools.* Tables 3.16 and 3.17 (see Reference No.10).

you solve yourself, modern books, comics, cooking, fishing, Enid Blyton etc. Other children wanted longer or different opening hours, more school-oriented/reference books, or more books 'for older readers'. Further suggestions included more tables and chairs, cassettes, and shelves.

'My idea of a good library is that it should have new books especially factual for students doing their homework.'

'Increase older readers section as adult library is *so* daunting in choice.'

'Hit the GLC for better hours.'

'More tables and space for children to do homework in.'

'I would like to see the library open later because sometimes you have to go after school.'

'More shelves, the books are overcrowded.'

'To be open more hours for kids at private school'.

'More helpers.'

'Less books, so easier to choose.'

'A bit bigger so that the books are not too crowded.'

'More copies of each book.'

'Having more information about school subjects also story books for teenagers.'

Very few of the suggestions were actually unreasonable, or impractical, though one or two perhaps were:

'Buy Marvel comics — hard to get in the shops and also costly.'

3.2.4 Library procedures/organization

The final general group of comments covered suggested changes in procedure and organization, again ranging over a wide variety of ideas. A few of the suggestions were quite censorious:

'Have the library cleaner.'

'Library should take more care over the books they have.'

A handful of others ranged from the frankly idiosyncratic to the exotic:

'I would like the clock put over the door.'

'Rearrange the library like a maze, one end children, the other end adults and you progress through it.'

Most of the suggestions centred around choosing, obtaining, or borrowing books, usually in terms of making it easier for borrowers to do these things — sometimes very literally:

'Books on top of the cases are too hard to reach for little people.'

Several children wanted 'older' or quiet area in the libraries and a few children wanted a say in book selection.

'The library should know who has what book.'

'More than four tokens.'

'Take out reference books for a limited time.'

'A poster on which children could write their recommendations like at school.'

'Teenagers should be allowed to use the adult library because there is nothing in the child section.'

'A quiet part and a talking part.'

'Have an under-fives corner.'

'Have a quiet section between 11 and 15 for a quiet read.'

'Find out which are the most popular books, get extra copies and also start selling books in the library.'

4 Reading scheme users

4.1 The children who use the schemes

Westminster's reading schemes are very popular, with a total of 1,447 children of all ages, enrolling in the schemes in 1981. The great majority of these children however are under 11 (eight was the peak age amongst all age groups in 1980). This year 463 of the enrolled on the schemes were aged 11 and over, of whom 90 were Bookworms, 180 Bookwizards, and 193 Bookmasters.

The schemes require a fairly sustained effort and amount of time to complete, and a fairly high proportion of children do not complete their scheme. The overall completion rate of masters and wizards was just over 50% in 1981, 65% for Bookworms, 60% for all scheme users together.

We asked the children on the schemes to complete side one of a further page of questions, for scheme users only, with side two designed to be filled in at completion of the scheme, or at a later date. Inevitably, as some children dropped out, the number completing questions on side two was considerably lower than questions on side one. This is why the total numbers vary between later questions. This chapter discusses responses to this final section of the questionnaire only. General aspects of library use among scheme users and non-users are discussed in Chapter Two. The total sample of scheme users was 312, of whom 60% completed their scheme. (For further details of methodology and sample, see Appendix 2.)

4.2 Publicity

The children were asked where they had heard about the scheme. The largest category of answers was via the branch librarian (see Table 4.1). The second most popular category was knowing it from previous use. In fact it seems likely that a proportion of these children originally heard about it from their librarians as well. Friends were the next main source of knowledge of the schemes, again begging the question of where the friends had heard of it in the first place. A further 10% mentioned school as a source of knowledge, five percent mentioned advertising and three percent mentioned parents or other members of their family.

21

Table 4.1 *Sources of knowledge of reading schemes: whole sample, boys/girls*

Sources of publicity	Total sample %	Boys %	Girls %
Librarian	35	38	33
School	10	8	11
Friends	10	8	10
Advertised	5	7	4
Knew it before	34	36	33
Parents	3	3	3
Librarians and friends	4	1	6
	N = 280	N = 90	N = 190

4.3 Previous scheme use

One-third of the children said they knew about the scheme from the previous year, although in fact, 70% of the children in the sample had taken part in a scheme previously, and of these children, the vast majority had used the scheme more than once before. It does seem that if the schemes appeal, they appeal strongly. Of the children who had used the schemes before, a quarter were using the schemes for the fourth, fifth or sixth time.

4.4 Non-completers

Children who did not complete their scheme were not singled out to be asked why, partly because it was expected that such children would be under-represented in the final sample. Interviewing did not start until the second week of the scheme, and as it seems probable that a high proportion of 'dropouts' do so on their first book it was thought that the final sample probably would not be representative of these children in particular.

This year, Bookwizard was introduced, as a scheme between Bookworm and Bookmaster using the top Bookworm list and requiring one review. This was intorduced at least partly to prevent children entering Bookmaster before they were ready for it, and does seem to have attracted some children away from it. Last year, 260 children enrolled in Boookmaster, this year 193 enrolled in Bookmaster and 180 in Bookwizard (aged 11 and over). However it is interesting to note that the completion rate for Bookmasters has remained unchanged, which may mean that the difficulty of the tasks required is not a major factor in whether the scheme entered is completed or not. At least one would have expected the completion rate for Bookmasters to rise, given the existence of an alternative socially acceptable scheme for the over-11s. (Bookworm is closely associated with young readers for many children.)

It is very possible that lack of time, or lack of awareness of time, is an important factor in failing to complete, and that this can vary from year to year with any one child. It may be therefore that there are two distinct groups of non-completers — the children who do not manage to finish in time and the children who consciously drop out, probably at a very early stage.

It was apparent that many children did not necessarily have a very clear idea as to how long six weeks really was, and that a visit from a cousin or a holiday away with mum and dad could disrupt their 'schedule' totally. The case studies indicated very strongly that the most committed scheme users were going to be the children who did not go away at all during the summer and who didn't like organized play activities very much (adventure playgrounds, summer play schemes, and so on). It is also interesting to note that when the children were asked what they particularly liked about the reading schemes, the most popular reply, given by 69% of all the children, was that they liked having something to do in the holidays. The case study children went to great pains at times to assure us that what they meant was that they liked having something to do that was interesting, the older ones in particular being very emphatic about refusing to take part in activities that didn't interest them and to a degree, didn't occupy them sufficiently. The girls in particular liked having something to do in the summer holidays.

4.5 Choice of reading scheme

The children were asked why they chose their particular schemes. Some of them interpreted this as a question on why they chose the library scheme in the first place, and answered in this unintended context.

The most popular reason given for joining the schemes at all was that it was something close to home, and indeed the vast majority of scheme users lived near to their branch libraries. The case studies indicated that even the older and more independent children were attracted to something close to home:

'A scheme for young people that sound interesting — close to home address' (17-year-old male scheme user).

In terms of the majority of children who indicated a reason for choosing their scheme in particular, Bookworms tended to feel that the other schemes were too hard or 'too old' for them. Bookwizards tended to feel that they were steering a middle course that was best suited to them and Bookmasters were happy to feel that they were using the scheme most appropriate to their age and status.

Bookmasters were likely to regard their scheme as challenging and were generally more positive in their reasons for choosing this scheme (see Table 4.2). For example, they were more likely to mention liking the books on their list, than the other groups of scheme users (see Tables 4.3 and 4.4).

Table 4.2 Reasons for joining Bookmaster

Stated reason	*No. of children*
Right level for me	34
Liked the books	29
Challenging — good for me	24
Like reviewing	8
Librarian said to	6
Done it before and liked it	6
Because done Bookworm before	4
Didn't know about others	2
Parents said to	1

N = 114

Table 4.3   Reasons for joining Bookwizard

Stated reason	No. of children
Right level for me	32
Wanted something different	18
Liked the books	15
Too old for Bookworm	9
Don't like reviewing	6
Librarian said to	3
Started before Bookworm	3
Easier than Bookmaster	3
Friends doing it	1

N = 90

Table 4.4   Reasons for joining Bookworm

Stated reason	No. of children
Easier than others	12
Don't like reviewing	6
Prefer the books	3
Because it is my first time on the scheme	3
Familiar with it	3
Didn't know about others	3
Teacher told me to	2
Other comments	5

N = 37

'Because it is fun when you have to write reviews and you can let out your feelings about the book. It is a challenge and something to do over the holidays also' (Bookmaster).
'Because I'm too old for the other schemes' (Bookmaster).
'I chose this scheme because I am not very good at writing book reviews' (Bookwizard).
'Bookworm too easy for me, Bookmaster too hard' (Bookwizard).
'Because I was on holiday a lot and so this was easier' (Bookworm).

One final point that should be made is that a lot of the children did not make a totally free choice. Great care is taken to try and ensure that parents did not unwittingly enrol their children in a patently unsuitable scheme but in fact there are various pressures directing children to particular schemes, such as the librarians themselves and the way the schemes are organized. It is obviously going to be far more satisfying for the children to enrol in a scheme that they can and do complete, rather than being unable to attend a presentation ceremony and receive a special certificate, and so on, and the librarians do tactfully try to direct children towards appropriate schemes, but without exerting undue or too obvious pressure.

At the same time, it seems very likely that the librarians have rather more indirect influence than perhaps even they are aware. So many children referred to their chosen scheme as being 'right for my age' or words to that effect, rather than in terms of preferring a particular list of books, that it is quite apparent that the way in which the schemes are described or introduced, can be very influential. Thus, fairly typical responses to the question why did you choose this particular scheme were:
'Because I am too old for the other schemes' (11-year-old Bookmaster).
'Because it is the right age group' (12-year-old Bookmaster).

Eleven has been designated as the official minimum age for enrolment in Bookmaster but of course this is not meant to imply that all 11-year-olds are 'too old' for other schemes. This is a problem that has been recognized by the introduction of Bookwizard this year, and it is too early to assess the full impact of Bookwizard as yet. It may be that very great care must be taken over the actual terminology used to describe the schemes and possibly that advertising a minimum age for Bookmasters is counterproductive. Alternatively it may be that Bookmaster should ideally be extended to include more than one set list, as with Bookworm, and be designated sole scheme for all over-11s.

4.6 Best-liked aspects of schemes

Ten aspects of the schemes were presented to the children and they were asked to indicate whether these aspects were liked a lot, quite liked, or were not at all important to them. They were also given the opportunity to mention anything they liked about the schemes that had not already been mentioned.

Table 4.5   Most liked aspects of the schemes: whole sample, boys/girls

Aspects liked a lot	Whole sample %	Boys %	Girls %
List of books to choose from	44	48	42
Someone to help me choose the books	27	31	25
Someone to talk to about the books	51	46	53
Badge	18	20	16
Certificate	48	61	41
Seeing my name up in library	32	41	27
Going to the presentation ceremony	53	59	50
Seeing my reviews published	47	58	41
Writing down my ideas about books	41	43	39
Having something to do in the holidays	69	62	72

N=168 N=307

In fact the best-liked thing about the scheme was that it provided something to do in the holidays (see also Section 4.4), with the girls being even more likely to agree with this than the boys. Only nine percent of the girls thought this was not important (see Table 4.6).

Amongst the boys, getting a certificate, going to the presentation ceremony and seeing their reviews published were close seconds to liking having something to do. Amongst the girls, having someone to talk to and going to the presentation ceremony were liked although not nearly as much as having something to do (see Table 4.5). Perhaps the girls do genuinely find it harder to occupy themselves in the summer holidays than the boys. The greatest percentage difference between the boys and girls was in liking certificates and badges (see Tables 4.5 and 4.6).

There is no doubt that girls in this age group tend to be more sophis-

Table 4.6 *Least important aspects of the schemes: whole sample, boys/girls*

Least important aspects of scheme	*Total sample* %	*Boys* %	*Girls* %
List of books	19	19	21
Someone to help me choose	52	48	54
Someone to talk to	31	27	30
Badge	62	50	73
Certificate	20	8	27
Name in library	43	39	45
Presentation ceremony	20	14	23
Review published	26	22	29
Writing down my ideas	19	16	20
Something to do in holidays	12	19	9

N=168 N=307

ticated than the boys, and it was noticeable that the girls were likely to be far more realistic — cynical even — in assessing their own interests and motives. This was particularly evident with Bookwizard. The boys simply said that they weren't very good at reviews, or the other books were too difficult for them. The girls (who are on average better readers than boys) often implied that one consideration when choosing Bookwizard was that they knew it was well within their capability to complete it without too much difficulty.

Other aspects of the schemes mentioned by the children, included liking reading the books and liking being introduced to new authors, both suggestions more likely to come from the girls than the boys.

4.7 Least-liked aspects of schemes

This was an open-ended question and the children seemed to find this harder to answer, although those that did answer seemed to have little difficulty expressing themselves.

Just over a quarter of the children answering this question (N=140) mentioned either not liking the books chosen or feeling that the choice was too restricted, usually in terms of being too old for them. This is not surprising insofar as most of the Bookmasters were under 14, whereas the books are intended for an 11 to 18 age range.
> 'Bookmaster books are quite boring — some are too grown up, e.g. Agatha Christie.'
> 'Most of the books are aimed at older readers, e.g. Goldfinger.'
> 'When I got the book I didn't like it put me behind, I thought I might not get through.'
> 'The list contained many books already read.'

It should be emphasized that all the children making these comments were nevertheless scheme users and most of them completed their schemes. Indeed it was likely to be the ones who read far more than their minimum required number of books, who complained about restricted choice. A smaller group of children mentioned disliking review writing, and some of the girls in particular felt there weren't enough copies of titles.
> 'Some books are on the list but you cannot get them because there are too few of them or they are just not there.'
> 'The thing I hated most about the Bookmaster was the reviews.'

One or two girls disliked waiting to be seen, or being questioned publicly, this was not something that any of the boys mentioned. The boys were more likely to dislike being restricted to one book a day, or feeling that they had insufficient time to complete their scheme.

'Did not have enough time — do not read very fast — went on holiday so could not read the right number.'

While some of these comments were worded fairly strongly there is no doubt that they were really only grumbles rather than serious complaints, although it may be that the children answering this final section of the questionnaire were largely committed scheme users. In fact, a quarter of the children answering this question said that there was nothing at all they disliked about the scheme.

'It's fine as it is, thank you very much.'

It may be noted that the DES[10] reported that while talking about books was by far the most popular activity as a follow up to writing, two-thirds of their sample expressed their dislike for writing about a book after reading it.

During the in-depth interviews with scheme users, a clear distinction was made by some children between review writing at school and review writing in the scheme — the biggest difference being that they were not being marked on the scheme, which made the entire exercise far more relaxed and enjoyable.

4.8   What would improve the scheme?

The children were asked to comment on what would make the scheme better for them, and once again, answers ranged over a variety of topics, not always in accordance with answers given to the preceding question, 'What did you least like about the scheme?'.

The largest group of answers (nearly 50%) was in terms of wanting more books, sometimes just left at that, sometimes detailing specific authors or types, or wanting 'better' books.

'More stories about real life ..... about crime ..... love ..... autobiography ..... horror ..... Grange Hill ..... bigger selection of titles to choose from ..... if they did not have so many books which were for older 16-year-olds.'

Other things mentioned by small numbers of children included wanting to be able to read more than one book a day, to have more copies of titles, longer loan periods and different testing times for different age groups, having easier books and including sequels in different schemes. At least 20 other different ideas were put forward by just one or perhaps two children, covering the usual range of imaginative, pragmatic and idiosyncratic.

'Have a dice-throwing game — you only have to answer questions if you do not throw above three, for example.'

'Bookmaster and Bookwizard list to be interchangeable. New schemes to make it more interesting — Bookraven and Bookeagle. Bookraven could be like Bookmaster but with synopsis to do on one of the books in addition. Instead of P, Y and M, lists should be given names, e.g. Bookcub, Bookfox, Bookwolf.'

'Properly coloured badges, e.g. blue and white.'

'Separate days and times for the very young and the more sensible readers on the scheme.'

'Would like fiction categorization of titles.'

'Useful to have an actual list of Bookmaster books to take away.'

'They should have a selection but if they don't like the selection they should be able to choose from another selection.'

'It would be better if you did Bookworm during winter holidays as well as summer because most people go on holiday during the summer and do not have a chance entering the Bookworm.'

'More advertisements, e.g. at Swiss Cottage.'

'Being able to do more than one book a day for people who want to do the scheme but are away a lot.'

5　Case studies of scheme users

These case studies are based on dossiers collected on a small group of 20 children, 10 of which are used here. The dossiers consisted of the children's questionnaires, a further tape-recorded interview (see Appendix 2 for interview schedule), reviews written by the children, and any further relevant comments made by the librarians who know the children.

Case studies — an informal qualitative approach — were deliberately used to complement formal questionnaires — a quantitative approach.

'Without doubt formal interviewing succeeds in achieving higher reliability than informal techniques. Reliability however is not everything. The other side of the picture is the validity of a response, that is its closeness to the truth which one is trying to ascertain ..... it may well be that the greater flexibility of an informal approach succeeds better than set questions in getting to the heart of the respondent's opinion.'[11]

In a three-month project, sights cannot be set unduly high and therefore only a small group of children could be used as case studies. Even so, it proved to be a useful, informative and interesting exercise. Useful because it was possible to make some checks on the validity of the answers given on the total questionnaires, informative because it added flesh to the bare bones of the answers on the questionnaires and most of all, interesting because it turned a 'respondent' into a real individual. In some ways, these case studies say more about scheme users than all the facts and figures found elsewhere in this report.

5.1　Judy: Bookmaster, aged 12

Judy is 12 and lives five minutes away from the branch where she enrolled as a Bookmaster. She is an old hand at the schemes, this is her fifth year and she was a Bookmaster the previous year. Judy completed her scheme, reading five books.

Judy has lived in London over five years, she is a regular Westminster junior library user. Her parents are library members, her mother is a school teacher. Judy listed 'parents' as her other source of books, and didn't agree with any of the problems we suggested library users faced (see Question 10 of questionnaire) and said 'I think this library is very good as it is now'. Amongst her reviews, Judy said:

Watch all night: 'Really liked because it was funny, sad, exciting and very true to life.'

Judy in love: 'Although I enjoyed this book it was like many others about teenage problems. I didn't like the simple style and the plot was so old and I guessed it straightaway. One good point though — some of the characters were very interesting because although they seemed to be happy and joking at everything, they were serious underneath.'

My mate Shofiq: 'This book was good though depressing. I thought the author handled the subject of racialism very realistically, showing how ignorant and superstitious many white people can be about coloured people's lives, and the book shows that race hate starts from childhood and is often picked up from parents.'

Later in her interview, Judy said this book had been the one she had most liked reading.

On her questionnaire, Judy had said that she liked funny stories, mysteries, and stories about teenagers like herself best of all, also that she would like the library to have more books by Judy Blume and John Rowe Townsend — 'books for teenagers and about teenagers'. During her interview, she said that she liked true to life books 'things that could really happen'. In general she preferred fiction, and books in the present, where something was happening. She remarked that she had 'got stuck' on an Agatha Christie that a friend had lent her — 'all the clues and things, just drags on, takes too long'. She also remarked that she had read *The Hobbit* at school with her class.

'I found it boring — most of our class found it boring ..... I don't like having books chosen for me and having to read it. I like being able to choose ..... I also don't like having to read out loud as we do at school.'

On her questionnaire, Judy had said that the following things were important to her when choosing a book: a good picture on the front cover; a good story; recommendations from other people; and, occasionally, having read a previous book by a particular author. When speaking to an interviewer she said that she did not find it easy to choose good books, and that she relied a lot on friends or her mother to recommend or choose for her. At school, her English teacher sometimes gave out reading lists which she liked — 'I like having a list, it helps you to choose'.

In the library, she said that occasionally an author's name caught her eye as she looked along the shelves, otherwise a cover would do so. She always read the blurb or a page of the book and looked at the chapter headings. In general she didn't like books that had chapter headings in fact.
'I don't know why, they sound easy.'
She was also very positive about how long a book should be.
'I like to read a lot of books and if there are about 200 pages, it means I can read a lot of books.'

Judy had said on her questionnaire that she knew of her scheme from the previous year, and that she chose Bookmaster again because it was 'recommended by librarian and teachers, and Bookworm books were getting too easy'. She particularly liked having a list of books to choose from, going to the presentation ceremony, seeing her reviews published and having something to do in the holidays, plus 'reading new books which I wouldn't have read otherwise'. She least liked writing the reviews and could not think of anything that would improve the scheme for her.

While being interviewed July said that she liked having discussions and liked talking about books.
'I have enjoyed Bookmaster because you have to read the books that are there and it introduces you to a whole new set of books that you might not read otherwise. I wouldn't have read any of the books except for *Noah's Castle* because I read books by John Rowe Townsend.'
She said that she liked reading the books and getting a certificate at the presentation ceremony, but not review writing.
'I found it even harder to write reviews last year so yes, the scheme has helped me to write them though I still prefer reading or talking.'
Judy said she did not think that the scheme had made her use the library any more than she would have done, or that it made her read any more books than she would have done normally in the summer but she did think that the scheme had introduced her to new authors.
'I hadn't heard of any of them except Joan Aiken. Normally I go for authors that I know in the library.'
At the same time, she said:
'When I got towards the end and had read all the books I

thought were the best, it got a bit difficult because I was left with ones I didn't like so much, and so it got harder', so that while she was prepared to try new authors, this didn't mean she could, or would, extend her reading range indefinitely.

Judy was characterized by her librarian as 'confident and an able reader'.

5.2   Annie: Bookwizard, aged 12

Annie is, at a state 'county' secondary school. Her second language at home is Cantonese, her family have lived in London for over five years. Her parents are not library members, Annie herself is a regular library user. Annie listed the school library as her other source of reading material and disagreed with all the suggested problems facing library users (Question 10). She couldn't think of any ideas to make the library better.

Annie was a Bookwizard, and had been a Bookworm three times before. The previous year she had read virtually one book a day for Bookworm but this year she read six books for Bookwizard and then stopped.

As a Bookwizard Annie only had to review one book and she had chosen *How to eat fried worms*. In a fairly short review she said:
'It is a good book because it was very exciting to get to the end to see if Billy does really do it. It is set in America, because you can tell because the people speak differently from the English.'

In her questionnaire Annie said that she liked art and craft books, funny stories, science fiction and stories about teenagers like herself. While being interviewed she said that best of all books she liked 'the funny ones and sort of about growing up'. She also said that she liked books with 'proper beginnings — books that start properly so you know what's happening from the beginning'.

She did not feel it was difficult to choose a good book.
'I just go round the shelves and when I see a good looking book I read a little bit of it, and when I see it's alright, I get it. I read the first bit and what it's about.'
She also looked at the pictures 'because pictures explain it better', and mentioned liking colourful covers. On her questionnaire Annie said the following things were important to her when choosing a

book: the print should not be too small; the book should not be too long; there should be enough illustration; reading the blurb; recommendations from other people. She said that when she read the back, or the first page, she was looking to see how exciting it was.
'If it is boring I just don't read it ..... if it is boring I can't get into it.'

Annie said that the reason she had stopped at six books this year was 'Because last time they had easier books — because I was with Bookworm, that's why sometimes I got from the easier shelf. The other books are harder'. She went on to say that it was not that the books this year on Bookwizard were too difficult but that:
'I didn't want to read them because some of them got boring ..... I read the first few pages at the library and then ..... I didn't understand it ..... it was boring so I put it back and got another one.'
Annie also said that she liked funny books and books about growing up, but there were very few like that on the Bookwizard list.

Annie said she had heard about her scheme from the librarian and had chosen it because 'Bookworm was too easy, Bookmaster too hard'. She liked having someone to talk to about the books, getting a certificate at the presentation ceremony, seeing her name up in the library, writing reviews and having something to do in the holidays. Most of all she had enjoyed writing her review and getting her certificate. She did not feel that the scheme had made her use the library more or read more books, particularly as she stopped at six scheme books this year, though she carried on using the library. She said that she enjoyed talking to the librarians about the book, but did not feel that the scheme had widened her reading.

On her questionnaire, Annie had said that her least liked aspect of the scheme was that it was too much like previous years (even though Bookwizard was a new scheme this year). She wanted 'something different instead of certificates — different organization — anything different from last year'. When interviewed she eventually said that she thought that different prizes should be given, rather than the same certificate, implying perhaps that she was a bit disappointed at finding that Bookwizard wasn't as different from Bookworm as she wanted it to be, or imagined it would be. Annie obviously had some problems with the Bookwizard list, it seems probable that for her the books were too mature, although she obviously felt that she had outgrown Bookworm. Bookworm children often read far more than the minimum number of books, because the books are easy to read and usually quite short on all the lists except the top one. It may be that for some children who move on to Bookwizard or Bookmaster, their expectations, initially, are too high.

Annie was a fairly quiet girl, one of four children and she said that there was nothing much else to do where she lived, apart from an adventure playground which she didn't like going to because 'it is a bit rough ..... and there are those boys ..... some of them bully me and make fun of me'.

5.3 David: Bookmaster, aged 17

David is 17, at a college of further education, a regular library member living near to his branch library, whose parents are not library members. David has lived in the area for over five years. He listed school library and buying himself as his other sources of books. He agreed that too many books were all words, that it was difficult to choose a book from all those on the shelves, and he did not understand how all the books were arranged. He said that in the library, he would have liked a more varied collection of music cassettes.

David was a Bookmaster for the first time this year, he had been a Bookworm the year before. He read six books.
> *Watch all night*: 'a gripping story set in London with mysterious characters, action and suspense ..... I recommend it to anyone who loves a cliff-hanging suspense thriller. I like the ending — like in real life a trail of debris will be left behind!'
> *Hitch-hikers guide to the galaxy*: 'The hitch-hikers guide will appeal only to people who like a story with a mixture of science fiction and comedy. Purists would probably dismiss it as a ridiculous yarn.'
> *History of Mr Polly*: 'H.G. Wells' novel of Mr Polly is a superb piece of literature, which not surprisingly was made into a television drama. It is a classic, brilliant story.'

One book David strongly disliked was:
> *Lucky Jim*: 'the story was pretty appalliing ..... set in a kind of public school, all the characters were, what I call weird ..... disillusioned ..... Jim doesn't know what he's doing half the time ..... I didn't enjoy it.'

David said he liked adventure stories, science fiction, ghost/horror and stories about teenagers. He also said that he liked 'real characters' — he hadn't greatly liked *Midnight is a place* because the characters seemed unreal. When he was asked why he liked science fiction — which isn't 'real' either, he said:

'but the gap between science fiction and science fact narrows every day — what is science fiction today becomes science fact tomorrow'.

David said he liked history, autobiography and also politics. He had enjoyed reading *Scarf Jack* — he liked the pace and the characters seemed real. Also he was impressed by the fact that 'the author obviously took a lot of time in writing it.'

David said the following things were important to him when choosing a book: print shouldn't be too small. book not too long; a good picture on the front; good titles; reading the blurb; a good story; and being a recent publication. He said initially that he didn't feel it was normally difficult to choose books though he qualified this later on.

'I just pick up books that appeal to my age group first of all ..... there's no one way ..... cover and illustrations don't interest me much ..... length doesn't matter ..... sometimes I look at the back of the book to get an idea what it's like ..... but you can't tell, a book can look appealing on the cover but when you read the first few chapters it may be totally boring ..... so sometimes it can be difficult.'

David didn't ever look for particular authors, though he said he liked to read something about the author. He reiterated his liking for new books 'if it's a new one I think, well, I'll try it'.

David had been a Bookworm the year before but he said he had enrolled as a Bookmaster after seeing it advertised, because:

'it was a scheme for young people that sounded interesting when advertised. It's close to home and no alternative scheme, also, the books are more suited to my age group.'

When asked if he was enjoying the scheme he said:

'it's alright ..... on the whole pretty good ..... some schemes the books are out of date or you can't get them, but not on this'.

He didn't approve of *Goldfinger* on the list.

'It's an old book and shouldn't really be there because it's a bit out of date, not a modern book.'

He thought that rather a lot of the books on the list appealed to 'slightly younger children' than himself, though on the whole it was quite a good list.

David did not think he had read any more books, or used the library any more than he would have done if he had not been on the scheme. He did think he had been tempted to read different authors, although by all accounts this was not an entirely successful exercise.

David was described as being very 'unusual, solitary and very sensitive'. He had a brother two years older than himself, and a younger sister.

5.4 Barbara: Bookmaster, aged 13

Barbara is 13, at a voluntary aided girls' school, a regular library user whose parents are public library members and who live near to their local branch. Barbara said that Tamil was her second language at home, her family had lived in London for over five years, and she listed the school library and friends as her other sources of reading material. She disagreed with four possible problems of library use but agreed that it was difficult to choose a book from all those on the shelves. Barbara did not have any ideas for making the library better for her.

Barbara was a Bookmaster. She had used the scheme three times before but this was her first year on Bookmaster. She read 24 books, reviewing most of them and enjoying the majority of them.
> *The Seven Dials mystery*: 'I thought this book was brilliant ..... I usually hate mysteries and I didn't think I would like it ..... I hope to read more Agatha Christie in the future.'
> *This school is driving me crazy*: 'I thought this was the best book I have read so far ..... very funny, explains everything very well ..... very realistic and fast moving.'
Later on, Barbara said that *My darling, my hamburger* was her favourite book of all.
> *Exeter blitz*: 'I enjoyed this book very much even though I thought it was better for boys to read than girls.'
> *Judy in love*: 'I like reading books about children of my age ..... this way I get to know what others of my age and older do ..... this is the type of book I normally like to read.'
Barbara didn't greatly like:
> *Rumble fish*: 'horrible descriptions', or
> *My mate Shofiq*: 'too much fighting', or
> *World zero minus*: 'difficult to get involved in ..... hard to believe the characters were human ..... I don't usually like sci-fi'.
She went on to say about *My mate Shofiq*:

'Page after page seemed to go on about some type of fight or argument. I don't think this type of bullying happens as much as it says in the book ..... as I go to a girls' school maybe the teasing is less but I still think the book is going too far.'
She didn't much like:
Under Goliath: 'maybe if boys read it, it would be more interesting ..... too much fighting ..... the main reason I didn't enjoy this book was because of the violence. I am sure if I was a boy I would have liked this book very much'.
She also didn't like:
Maybe I'm amazed: 'there wasn't any sense in any of the stories, half the time I didn't know what was going on.'

On her questionnaire Barbara said that she liked art or craft books, love stories, school stories and stories about teenagers like herself. She said she would have liked the library to have more cookery books and more stories about teenagers. When being interviewed she remarked that she had read *Gulliver's travels* in class.
'It was alright as a class book but I wouldn't have chosen it ..... I like reading stories about children of my age and particularly people who live in this country, though I like American stories as well.'
At school, Barbara's teacher issued lists of books that they would enjoy or should read and then they picked out books from the list, at the school library. Barbara 'looked for books about people like myself and school stories'. She also mentioned that she really liked Judy Blume — she had read every story written by her, and enjoyed them 'because they are about children like me and all the troubles they have at school and all the family life'. Barbara wasn't interested in non-fiction, science fiction or horror stories, and she didn't like reading detailed descriptions of fighting.

Barbara listed the following things as being important when choosing a book: good picture on the front; reading the blurb; book shouldn't be too short; and a good story. She said that she did not usually find it wasy to choose books:
'because there's such a lot of books ..... you go round looking at the shelves and you can't just pick one out of the whole thing. During school term I ask the school librarian to help me find a few books'.
In the public library she found her own books however, picking out appealing titles and/or covers to start with.
'If it's got a horrible picture, or just writing on the front, then it doesn't really appeal.'

She always reads what was written on the back of the book and always reads the first page. She did not like books that had long pages full of description, she liked conversation.

Barbara said that she did not have much to do in the holidays and that she liked reading the books best of all about the scheme. This was the first year she had done Bookmaster, 'it was a bit harder but alright'.

Barbara was used to review writing, at school she had library lessons where the class went into the library to submit their reviews to the teacher or read them out loud.
  'I don't mind writing reviews but I like to hear what other people have got to say.'
In fact Barbara's reviews were noticeably mature and she was able to say why she liked or disliked a book in concise but expressive terms.

Barbara did not think she would have used the public library as much if she had not been on the scheme.
  'I don't usually take out a lot of reading books because I get them from school.'
She also did not think she would have read quite as many books.
  'Because I joined this it kind of made me determined I had to read a few books and so I came here every day.'
And finally, she did feel that she had been persuaded to read rather different books from those she read normally.
  'You've only got a small amount of books to choose from and the first 10 I read were all the books I liked. The others I didn't really think I was going to enjoy but ..... there was an Agatha Christie book I didn't think I would like but I had to take it out and I found that I really liked it ..... so quite a few of the books there I found I really liked afterwards.'
At the same time, Barbara had felt restricted towards the end.
  'Then there's all those horrible books you don't want to read and you've got to read because otherwise you'll have to stop and there's not much else to do during the holidays.'
There's no doubt that for some of the girls in particular, how to occupy themselves pleasantly, was a real problem!

Barbara was characterized as being 'able and open'.

5.5   Peter: Bookworm, aged 13

Peter is 13 and lives in Eire. In the summer he visits his cousins who live on the housing estate near to the branch used by Peter and his cousins. Peter said that his parents were not public library members.

Peter's girl cousin was enrolled on the scheme, initially as a Book-wizard and then as a Bookmaster. His cousin was said by their branch librarian to enjoy the competitiveness of the scheme. Peter was persuaded largely by his cousin to join a scheme. He enrolled in Bookworm and read five books. As soon as he had completed the required number of books, his librarian noted that he borrowed exclusively non-fiction, mostly about Ancient Greece, or the Romans.

Peter agreed that too many books in the library were too hard to read and that it was difficult to choose a book from all the books on the shelves and also that he did not understand how all the books were arranged.

Peter did not need to write any reviews for his scheme. On his questionnaire he listed stories about famous people, history, mysteries and war stories as being his favourite types of books, and he would have liked the library to have had more war books and more history books. When interviewed, he emphasized his liking for history books and books about war. He also said that he liked 'books about something that I'm going to learn about in the future', and 'books about other countries'. He said that at his school:
> 'we only have Ladybird books and we read them every Friday and we can take them home'.

Peter did not find it easy to finish his scheme but he kept going and was satisfied at succeeding in completing it, although it was noticeable to his librarian that he was relieved to get to the end of it. He was quite impressed by the range of books available to him.
> 'I enjoyed doing Bookworm because there's a good range of books and I liked that.'

Peter listed the following things as being important when choosing a book: print shouldn't be too small; book not too long; enough illustrations; a good picture on the front cover; a good title; paperback; a good story. He said that he didn't normally find it difficult to choose books in the library although he talked entirely in terms of choosing non-fiction.
> 'If it's history or something I would look at the first few pages

..... I like colourful pictures in books about battles and things ..... the bigger the book the better ..... I don't mind as long as there is a lot of pictures in them.'

Peter said on his questionnaire that the best parts of the scheme for him: were having a list to choose from; having someone to help him choose; talking about the books; going to the presentation ceremony; and having something to do in the holidays. He said that he liked talking about the books best.

'I liked being asked a lot of questions.'
He couldn't think of any improvements he wanted to see to the scheme.

'This is my first time and I enjoyed it. it's alright ..... but reading five was quite enough.'
Peter eventually volunteered that he had chosen his fifth book very carefully, in order to be sure of 'passing': 'It was kind of a little bit easy'. In fact he need not have felt at all guilty, he did persevere even though he was obviously stretched somewhat. It was noticeable that the girls rarely put themselves in this situation. They tended to be better readers than the boys but they also tended to choose schemes that they were sure of completing.

5.6 Sara: Bookmaster, aged 14

Sara is 14, a regular library user whose parents are library users. Sara's family is of Indian origin, they live close to their branch library and have lived in London for over five years.

Sara listed the school library and friends as being her other sources of books and disagreed with all the potential problems facing library users. She was a Bookmaster and had entered the scheme once before, also as a Bookmaster. She had read 15 books and reviewed most of them.

Her favourite book had been:
  Walkabout: 'put in that situation I think I would have acted in much the same way as she did ..... having a little sister myself I can understand how she feels.'
She also read:
  Sky girl: 'although I was doubtful about taking it out I liked the way everything was clearly written and there were no long boring descriptions ..... it ended properly and did not leave me wondering what's going to happen next.'

The incredible journey: 'although I love animals I usually don't like reading books about them but this was an exception ..... it was very exciting and easy to read and it finished properly.'
This school is driving me crazy: 'this book was very enjoyable from beginning to end ..... this could have been double the size because it is so enjoyable that you just have to keep reading on ..... I would really like to read more books by the same author.'
My mate Shofiq: 'it was sad and thoughtful but good with plenty of conversation. Nothing seemed to finish off properly though, it needed another.'
Kes: 'Billy was 15 but came across more as an 11 year old ..... too much bad language in this book and some sections were boring.'

Sara did not much like a collection of ghost stories.

'I think this is more suitable for people who are older than I am.'

On her questionnaire Sara had said that she liked ghost/horror stories but when interviewed she qualified this. She did like them, but not all of them, because she did not always like the author's style of writing, particularly as the vocabulary was often too difficult, and also because they were often 'more of a story than really being very scary'. Of the one book on the scheme that she had really disliked, she said:

'This must be about the most boring book I have ever read in all my life. I didn't understand who was saying what in most stories ..... the stories didn't have proper endings ..... each one was worse than the one before.'

Apart from ghost stories, Sara had said that she liked school stories and stories seen on television, and, also, that she would like the library to have more cookery books. She also said that the following things were important to her when choosing books: the print shouldn't be too small; book not too long; good title; reading the blurb; seeing the story on television; paperbacks; recommendations from other people. She didn't find it too difficult to choose books normally.

'I read the back or the inside where a little is written about the book and read bits out of it ..... and I'm not usually wrong about what I think I like.'

She looked through the book for, 'quite a bit of conversation and no boring descriptions'.

Sara emphasized that she did not like print that was too small or too large, she didn't like space stories or non-fiction, 'usually too small print'. At school, she liked reading in class but not when everyone read the same book to themselves quietly.

'Because we all end up at different levels and I feel uncomfortable when I'm only in the middle and someone's ahead of me.'
She had read *Kes* at school, and had chosen it again on the scheme.
She said she enjoyed it more the second time round though her
review showed that she still had reservations about it. Sara said
that the things she most liked about her scheme were having a list
of books to choose from, going to the presentation ceremony and
having something to do in the holidays. She would have liked to
have seen more books on the list.

'Not any specific kind of books, just more ..... the choice was
quite good but there were too few.'
She would also have liked to have been able to take out more than
one book at a time.

'Because it's a little bit difficult sort of going to the library,
running back and forth ..... and they could have had more
copies of the books so that there would always be one for the
next person.'
(Sara had noted books to take out next time, which weren't there
next time.)

Sara enjoyed the competitive element of the scheme and said that
she also enjoyed reading 'set books instead of looking round in the
library ..... it's a nice scheme I think'. She thought the scheme had
made her read books more thoroughly, in one go rather than piece-
meal.

'I would have read books but I wouldn't have read them solidly
..... I'd have only read a bit ..... but then I decided, oh well I'm
going to read them all in one go so that it's fresh in my mind to
write the review.'
She also remarked on the fact that feeling obliged to complete a
book sometimes had its rewards.

'I took out *Who's Bill* and started reading it and then it wasn't
very interesting so I thought, well, I've got it out now I might
as well finish it ..... and then I was pleased that I did.'

She quite liked writing her reviews. She wrote reviews at school but
preferred these ones.

'At school we have to write a basic story line but here I
could take my time more about it and flick through the book
and I thought of quite a lot to say ..... it was nice writing a
review here.'
Sara mentioned that she had barely read the minimum number of
books the year before, because she had started halfway through and

had not had the time. This year she read 15 and had stopped only because she found it increasingly difficult to choose books 'because you had read the cream of the books first'.

Sara was described by her librarian as being mature and sophisticated.

5.7 Helen: Bookmaster, aged 16

Helen is 16, at school and she had just sat for her 'O' level exams. She is an old hand at the schemes and was enrolled in Bookmaster, which she had enrolled in the year before as well. She apparently never filled in the first section of the questionnaire although there was a completed final section relating to scheme use, that she had filled in.

Helen lived near to the library and she told us that she had one sister 'who goes away in the holidays and I'm usually by myself but it doesn't bother me — I like to be by myself. I find things to do'.

Helen had read and reviewed 16 books, writing very long reviews, much given to hyperbole and including long detailed blow-by-blow accounts of the plots.

Emma and I: (this was her favourite one) 'This touched the parts of my heart only before reserved for momentous occasions — this to me was one of them ..... only one other book I have read did the same to me (A kiss through glass by Shirley Nolan) ..... more books like this please ..... real life experiences are so much more interesting than stories.'

My darling my hamburger: 'very funny ..... I really enjoyed it ..... it's not the first time I read it but it gets funnier as you read it ..... the characters were very true to life ..... yes, a firm 'yes' to all libraries in England ..... if this book is anything to go on, Pardon me you're stepping on my eyeball, Confessions of a teenage baboon and The caretaker's gone bananas will be as fantastic and interesting as this one was.'

Judy in love: 'I enjoyed this book ..... Judy was a fantastic character, warm, friendly, funny but the book was a little one-sided and told almost only Judy's feelings — more could have been said about her parents' feelings and attitudes.'

Watch all night: 'This book is everything you could want — mystery, intrigue, romance, travel, excitement ..... this book deserves a medal for explaining how the nuclear race is, to people like myself, who don't understand all the scientific language they use.'

The Exeter blitz: '..... very descriptive ..... I disagree with the feeling that this book was just for boys ..... This book was also educational and would aid anyone, like myself, who studied world wars at school. David Rees must have done a lot of research to complete this book.'

Helen wasn't too keen on *The Lord and Mary Ann*:

'Although the book was very good, the Mallens' trilogy were very much the same and you could guess what would happen ..... I don't think everybody would like this type of book. I don't usually read them but seeing as I had to, I read it. Never before have I read any of Catherine Cookson's novels and I approached this one with caution — I am not becoming hooked!'

When interviewed Helen said she liked nursing romance books, particularly by Lucille Andrews. She also liked Agatha Christie — so far.

'But I like a lot of junior authors ..... I like Enid Blyton ..... I was always an Enid Blyton fan and I was really upset when I found out that she had died in about 1945 ..... I still like her books even though they are ..... well they are not really childish, they've got grown ups in them as well, but they are good. They show children as children ..... the children get dirty, they get told off, she doesn't put them in any class of their own. They show children in real life which is what I like.'

At school, Helen said:

'Usually the teacher will recommend books to read over the holidays to help with our studies, but the storybooks are mainly for the older readers, say 14 or 15, like the Brontë sisters, Jane Austen or Mrs Gaskell. I don't really like those, I prefer nowadays, stories of nowadays, not long ago. Twentieth century not 19th or 17th. Our sociology teacher gave us a list of 30 books all about society today and they were very interesting.'

Helen also said that she was 'into murders ..... I've just taken out the *Murderer's who's who* — it sounds horrible but it's like the 'Ladykillers' series on TV ..... that was good as well'. She didn't like science fiction and she didn't think that she would like Joan Aiken books, 'It's not science fiction but ..... it doesn't appeal to me', though in fact she did like *Midnight is a place* by Joan Aiken, 'but it helped to see it on the TV, to see the people act it out'.

Helen didn't usually find it difficult to choose good books.
'I always read the first chapter anyway to see if it's a good book but most of the books in the library are good, especially the books for older readers. I like a colourful cover, it does more to attract you than a dull one ..... I like the picture to tell you something about the story ..... length doesn't really matter but it would have to be say, over 100 pages, because otherwise it's far too quick. The chapter headings sometimes help because they tell you roughly what's going to be happening, which is what they should do. I look at the back and read a couple of pages and I look to see what the papers have said about it ..... If it's "fantastic — *Sunday Times*" then you know it must be good.'

Helen really liked 'Topliners', a publisher's series. She had written to the series' editor asking for a complete list of titles and to say how much she had enjoyed the one she had read, 'it appealed to me very much being a teenager myself'.

Helen said she had enjoyed the scheme this year although the previous year she had only read one book.
'I think it was just my frame of mind — I had a lot of people about me. My friends used to come over quite frequently ..... I'd hurt myself and I wasn't too interested in anything and I couldn't be bothered really, But this year I've had nothing to do and my sister has been away for six weeks so I was really by myself and I wanted something to do. I enjoy having a list to go by — they must obviously be good books because otherwise they wouldn't have recommended them to you.'

On her questionnaire, Helen said that she particularly liked writing down her ideas about books and having something to do in the holidays. Not only did she like writing reviews but also thought it was good practice.
'When you are younger it is easeir to talk to someone but when you're older I think it's better for you to write it all down. Not only does it aid you with your school but it aids you with your vocabulary as well.'
She also liked discussing her reviews with the librarians.
'They can bring out more things in you ..... they say why did you say that, whereas you can't say to yourself, why did I put that down.'
Helen wrote reviews at school but saw them rather differently.
'It's very much laid down what you say and what you don't say

..... you write what the teacher wants you to write really .....
you can criticize but you have to be able to really back it up .....
here, you have to say why but not in such detail ..... you're not
being marked on it.'
Helen remarked that some of her set English books at school she did
not like at all, particularly the period ones, 'especially one about
India in the 1880s — so boring'. On the other hand *The Crucible* was
'fantastic', and so was the play when the class went to see it.

Helen said she was not at all interested in any of the 'carrots'
involved in the scheme — badges, certificates, ceremonies,
published reviews etc. However she did feel there were not enough
librarians — a visit could take half a day. She wanted to have 'one
librarian for Bookworm and one for Bookmaster, and each sticking
to their own scheme', though she hastened to add 'it takes a long
time but they do a good job and I'm glad they do the Bookmaster'.

Helen did not think that using the scheme had made her use the
library more or borrow any more books but she did feel that she had
been introduced to some new authors, and that she had actually
read, more books, from start to finish.
'I would have got books but I wouldn't have read them or I
would have just flicked through them. But on the scheme you
have to read the whole book and you get a lot of things out of
the books, they teach you a lot of things as well, which helps
you and they are just very good books which they choose for
you.'

She was able to remember the authors of nearly all the books she
had read on the scheme, unlike many of the younger children, and
had usually looked for other titles by authors she had liked. She was
also quite positive about authors she liked generally. She picked out
The Exeter blitz in particular as a book she would not have normally
read.
'I only took it because I had to get one at that minute and
didn't have any time to choose. But it was good and I'm glad I
got it now.'
Helen, like several other scheme users, commented that she had
picked out some books she had read before, but, as with the other
scheme users, this didn't bother her.

Helen was characterized as 'friendly and easy to talk to but not as
confident as she sounds'.

5.8   Ben: Bookwizard, aged 12

Ben is 12, and lives with his parents within walking distance of his branch library. Ben's parents are Jamaican, they have lived in London for over five years. They are not public library members. Ben is, he is a regular library user. He enrolled on his first scheme, Bookwizard, this year, reading five books and writing one review. Ben listed the school library as his other source of books to read and agreed that too many books in the library were too long, too many books were too hard to read and that too many books were all words.

Ben's review, of *Grumble's yard*, largely restated the plot and did not really indicate his feelings about the book though he said later that,

'I liked it when they had fights ..... that's really funny you know ..... it sort of tells you how they had a fight and everything like that.'

He also said that his favourite scheme book had been *How to eat fried worms* — this was funny and he liked the way they explained things.

Ben said he liked funny stories, ghost/horror stories, adventure stories and sport stories best of all, and he wanted the library to have more 'general knowledge and funny stories'. In his interview he said that he liked books on space and on 'mechanics ..... about working on cars and everything ..... and electricity ..... fixing things'. He also liked Kung Fu stories and books about people in the present — time stories, people talking about their lives. He liked reading about things that happened in school 'because it warns you about the sort of things that could happen', and about gangs 'because it sort of explains how they have fights and everything and you end up getting yourself involved'.

Ben said that usually he took out books that would only take about an hour or so to read, so he could take a few at a time, and usually 'books that could benefit you ..... I could learn about something'. It seemed that he did not read a great deal of fiction normally. He said that he read novels at school but preferred books on fixing things, sometimes he took out storybooks from the library during the year but not very many.

On his questionnaire Ben had listed the following items as being important in choosing a book: print shouldn't be too small; book not too long; enough illustrations; good titles; seeing the story on TV; and a good story. In his interview, he said that he didn't always find it easy to choose good books.

'First of all a quite good cover sometimes attracts me ..... then you start to read it and you say that's good but sometimes it's not.'

He did not usually read the blurb, 'sometimes ..... not really', but he usually read a little bit of the books, to see if it was going to be exciting.

Ben said he had heard of the scheme from friends.

'I was bored at home and my friend said Bookworm was here and could I come along with him ..... so I came along a few times ..... and then I started on a library book. First I was a Bookworm and then he said would you like to be a Bookwizard because you get a higher certificate, and I said yes. It wasn't all that boring and so I did it and then I stopped a week because there were games at Harlesden and I could play, like cricket, then I came back again. Actually I liked it because you can have a set number of books and you say how you enjoyed them or didn't enjoy them ..... I liked talking about the books more than the writing ..... if you just read it and finish it, you don't get to understand it but when you read it and talk about it and understand it, you sort of think, oh this is a really good book.'

Ben said he had done reviews at school, though writing obviously was not his strongest point and he had not enjoyed doing his review. He had enjoyed the talking part though — he had interviewed people in the street, asking them what they thought of the area, as part of a school project and had greatly enjoyed that.

Ben had not started on the scheme at the beginning of the holidays, and was a bit pushed to finish in time. He did not think he would have been in the library nearly as much if he had not been on the scheme, 'it sort of brings me out', and he did not think he would have read so many books, 'not really, no, I'd be out playing'. He found it difficult to say whether he had read any different types of books on the scheme, possibly because he did not normally read much fiction at all. He said that he had mostly chosen funny stories in the Bookwizard list and had enjoyed all the five books he had read. He tended to think of libraries as boring because 'you just read and that's all you do' whereas he liked to talk — and therefore Bookwizard 'hadn't been all that boring'. Ben was all for introducing activities into the library — including games (excluding chess, which was played in the library already).

Solitary reading was obviously too passive an activity for Ben really to be able to enjoy. The opportunity to talk about what he had read was what actually kept him on the scheme.

5.9 Andrea: Bookwizard and Bookmaster, aged 12

Andrea is 12 and lives on the large housing estate close to her local library. She enrolled as a Bookwizard but went on to do Bookmaster as well. She has used the schemes five times already, last year as a Bookmaster. This year she tried Bookwizard first, because it was something new, but went on to read a total of 22 books from both lists. Andrea's family have lived in London for over five years, her parents are public library members and she is a regular library user.

Andrea listed 'friends' and 'buying herself' as her sources of books, other than the library, and of the suggested problems facing library users, only agreed that it was difficult to choose a book from all the books on the shelf. She also said that she wanted the library 'to organize the books better, and have activities going on'.

Andrea wrote quite a number of reviews.
Sky girl: 'I enjoyed this a lot ..... definitely a girl's book.'
Maybe I'm amazed: 'I didn't enjoy this book much — mainly because of the way they speak. It makes it hard to understand what they are saying. All the stories seemed to consist of kids smashing things up, or moaning about something which was their own fault. Most of them had wasted their own time at school, or not even going to school.'
This school is driving me crazy: 'Parts of this were very true to life and I think that was why I enjoyed it.'
Judy in love: 'I enjoyed this mainly because it was realistic especially having parents like Judy ..... I would recommend this and call it a girl's book because boys wouldn't like a story like this.'
Rumble fish: 'I can't say I enjoyed this because stabbing people and stealing isn't very pleasant ..... I think the only normal person in this story was Steve who had a bit of common sense. I must admit that this is true to life, but only in America ..... I don't think it was worth writing a book like this because I think it encourages more people to act like this ..... I think this book is more suitable for boys than girls.'

One of the gang: 'I didn't think very much of this book ..... the ages jumped so that stories didn't go in the right order ..... not very well organized or well written ..... I don't think you should go along with everything the gang do ..... you should make the most of what you yourself like doing.'

Emma and I: (an autobiographical account of a guide dog and her blind owner who later regained her sight) 'I really enjoyed this book very much ..... I couldn't stop reading it.'

On her questionnaire, Andrea had said that she liked adventure stories, animal stories, school stories and stories about teenagers like herself, although she qualified this slightly when interviewed.

'I like reading about children of my own age but sometimes, in books, they are always writing problems and you get a bit sick of that.'

Andrea felt that the following things were important to her when choosing a book: print shouldn't be too small; book shouldn't be too long; reading the blurb; and that the story should seem interesting. She did not feel she had too much trouble choosing books in practice though she had agreed on her questionnaire that this was a problem.

'I usually have a good look through and I read a little bit of the book to make sure I can understand it ..... sometimes if a friend has read the book, I go and get that book to see what it's like, and really, you can tell what books you are going to like from the description in it ..... I think a really dull cover does put you off.'

She also said that the blurb was not as important to her as actually reading the first few pages, 'and if I don't like it, I don't take it'.

Andrea expressed very little interest in non-fiction, 'only if I need it for school work'. She felt that boys took out non-fiction, girls took out fiction.

Andrea said that she had liked getting her certificate, seeing her name up in the library and seeing her reviews published. She was critical of the Bookwizard selection but preferred this year's Bookmaster selection to last year's.

One of the reasons she had tried Bookwizard this year was, she said, because she hadn't greatly liked the Bookmaster books last year, 'they all seemed to be really older books for older children'. This year she thought there was a better variety of books though 'a lot seemed to come from up North, with accents' which she did not like.

She felt that the requirements were too lax.

'Instead of four or five you should have to read about seven because otherwise it's too easy ..... some people go on a lower age group and they know they can read that easily and then get fed up.'

Andrea did not think she would have used the library as much if she had not been on the schemes, 'there would have been no need, I've got plenty of books at home'. While she therefore did not think she had read any more books than she would have done, she did think that she had read different books. She remarked that she would have read 'mainly Enid Blyton books' and was quite emphatic that, for example, she would never have chosen a book such as *Emma and I*, which was her favourite one on the schemes.

Andrea also made a point of saying that she liked the kind of questions put to her about the Bookmaster books.

'In Bookwizard they just ask you what the story is, in Bookmaster they ask you all different kinds of questions.'

She was fairly non-committal about review writing, regarding it as a chance to practise something she was occasionally required to do at school.

'My English teacher sometimes gives a book for homework to take home, read so many chapters and then write about. So Bookmaster gives you a bit of practice ..... it helped me last year when I first started secondary school ..... it's because you are asked different questions, not just what happened in the books.'

Andrea had managed to choose 22 books from the Bookwizard and Bookmaster list after a while because:

'they were different types to what I'd read before ..... some of them were about gang problems and I saw that a lot of them were about old-fashioned times and I don't read those books a lot really.'

On the other hand she said that she went on to Bookmaster because after reading about 10 Bookwizard books, there was not much variety left.

She recounted, rather disapprovingly, that:

'one librarian said these books (Bookwizard) were a bit babyish for me, but I enjoyed it, so ..... I don't know why she was complaining about it.'

In fact, the Bookwizard books were undoubtedly a little young for her — she was characterized by her librarian as very serious, with strong likes and dislikes, writing mature reviews. She was said to be encouraged at home to do the scheme and to be doing Bookmaster because her mother tells her it is good practice. Andrea herself was very positive about the fact that she would not have been doing it if she did not enjoy it. She said that she didn't have a lot to do in the summer holidays though her mum and dad took her out from time to time. She didn't like going to playcentres — 'I like doing things on my own'.

5.10 William: Bookmaster, aged 11

William is 11, a regular library user who lives on the large estate close to his branch library, with his mother. William is partly West Indian, his brother and sister live out of London with his father. His mother is a public library member who has lived in London for over five years. William was a Bookmaster for the first time this year, but he had been a Bookworm several times before.

William listed the school library as his other source of books, he attended a boarding school. He agreed that it was difficult to choose a book from all the books on the shelves in the public library and yet wanted the library to have 'more of each book, more of each kind of book and more of each author'.

William read twelve books. His two absolute favourites were:
One of the gang: 'a very true to life story ..... very descriptive .....
I liked the characters ..... I liked the part about the fights .....
and when they try to live in the woods', and
My mate Shofiq: 'this was the best book I have ever read ..... it
makes you feel really, really happy and really, really sad ..... it
is about the troubles that happen between Pakistanis and
white people ..... I like the way Shofiq *nearly* always stays calm
..... it is detailed and brilliantly written and that is all there is
to say.'
William also liked:
The Exeter blitz: 'a very exciting story ..... about the bombing on
May 1942 of Exeter. I liked this story because it is an interesting story about World War Two.'
This school is driving me crazy: 'very enjoyable ..... in some parts
rather amusing in other parts rather violent ..... very true to
life.'
Hitchhikers guide to the galaxy: 'the way Douglas Adams writes

is truly marvellous ..... in this book the impossible is suddenly possible ..... very comical.'

Rumble fish: 'a brilliant story set in America ..... it sounds true to life ..... Rusty James has to fight his way through life to defend his reputation for being the toughest in the neighbourhood ..... brilliantly written.'

The incredible journey: 'a very exciting book in which death approaches nearly every chapter ..... there was never one part in the book when the story was just slightly boring ..... I particularly liked the story because it was not like most of the other soppy animal stories when you have animals speaking like humans.'

Under Goliath: 'very fast moving ..... lots of action ..... Goliath is a giant crane exported from Germany to the troubled city of Belfast ..... the story is about the teenagers of the city and the goings on there ..... it was very exciting the whole book.'

William was less enthusiastic about:

Maybe I'm amazed: 'I think this book was too old for me ..... quite a good book but the thing I didn't like was the way the author used "t" and "tha" and other things — sometimes it was hard to understand what the person was saying.'

Walkabout: 'a detailed and descriptive book ..... probably suitable for 12 to 15 year olds.' (William was 11.)

William said he liked science fiction, ghost/horror, school stories and stories about teenagers best of all, and these were the types of books he would like the library to have more of. When interviewed he said that he liked animal stories

'that aren't actually making the animals talking like humans because otherwise it's a bit babyish. In *Animal Farm*, although they have them talking it's not really about the actual animals, it's about the Russian Revolution and the animals represent the people ..... I really like sort of real stories ..... something to believe.'

During the year William said he tended to read:

'just reference books, encyclopaedias I am reading ..... because we have to have reading books all the time at school, but reference books ..... if I find I haven't got anything in my mind, I just have a look at reference books.'.

William listed the following items as being important when choosing a fiction book: book shouldn't be too long; good picture on the front; good title; reading the blurb; and a good story. He said he

had read books that did not look so good from the outside but which turned out to be very good in fact, so he did not necessarily worry too much about the covers of a book. He said he always read 'the introduction'.
'If I like the introduction I might get it, and sometimes I flip through it.'

On his questionnaire he had said that it was difficult to choose good books but when interviewed he preferred not to commit himself to this point. The overall impression gained was that he did not normally use either his school or the public libraries fiction collection very much at all. Though he was at boarding school he did use the public library in the holidays.
'I find it quite easy (to choose books from the public library) but I think if there was, say, two copies of each book, that would be a lot better because when one of them is away you have to reserve it and I reserved one about four weeks ago and it hasn't come up yet.'
During the year, he said that:
'sometimes I just like reading quite easy books like the Asterix books or I might like to read science fiction say ..... If I can remember some of the authors I look for them.'
He also said that he would only ask the librarians for help 'if there's a particular one I want to read but that's only about twice a year'.

William remarked that it had taken him three days to read *Border kidnap*, although he said he was usually a fast reader, because he had had so much to do in the holidays — he was at his dad's house at the time. He said:
'usually I find I've got a lot of things after school like playing football which sort of takes my mind off it and I forget to read and so it takes me about a week and a half to read a book'.

For William, the best part of his scheme was reading the books, followed by writing the reviews. On his questionnaire, he had not felt able to list anything he 'liked a lot' about the scheme, but gave the fact that he liked doing book reviews as his reason for entering the scheme. He was used to review writing at school, and said 'when you have to write about it, it helps you to understand the book', and indeed he was rather good at review writing.

William felt that there had not been quite enough books on the scheme, and least liked the one-book-a-day rule. He would have liked at least to have been able to take out two books at a time:

57

'also you can only do one review a day and some of the books I read, I read quite quickly and when I finished there wasn't anything else to do'.

He did not really feel he had been introduced to new authors, largely because he did not tend to notice the authors anyhow, but he did think he probably would not have read as many books in such a short space of time. He did say that he did not often have as much free time as he had at the moment, certainly not during term time. He did not like going to playcentres in the summer he said, and when he was not visiting his father, he got bored, 'Bookmaster helped me not to be bored'.

He would have liked to have seen more fiction books in Bookmaster, within his range.
'I don't think there were many science fiction books I could actually understand, I only saw one.'
In fact he had read that before anyhow.
'But I wanted to read it again and then I realised there wasn't Part 2 of it in the Bookmaster section — so I found that a bit disappointing.'

When asked whether he thought being on the scheme had helped him over the years, to get to know his librarian better, William answered, rather disarmingly:
'Sometimes, you find out what sort of books they like.'

6 Book preferences

Two questions were specifically asked about book preferences. The first was:
> 'What kind of books do you like most of all?'

and suggested 18 possible categories. The children could, and did, list 'other' categories. The second question asked:
> 'What kind of books would you like us to have more of?'

This was completely open-ended and was in effect a re-wording of the first question but without the constraints of pre-listed categories of answers. While a relationship in the way the two questions were answered was apparent, there were differences in responses.

6.1 Preferred categories

In the sample as a whole, the best liked categories were funny stories, mysteries, ghost/horror and adventure (see Table 6.1).

The DES[12] found that in response to the open statement 'I wish that books .....', 25% of their sample wanted more action and adventure, plus another 50% wanted books to be more 'thrilling or mysterious', plus another nine percent wanted more funny stories. In answer to the question on what kind of books the library should have more of, eight percent mentioned funny stories, 26% mentioned adventure and mysteries (see Table 6.2).

The Southgate Report[13] made some interesting observations about preferred reading, although discussing seven to nine year olds only. It concluded, after looking at books actually chosen by the children, that in general:
> 'humorous books were often preferred to other types, that the above average readers out-numbered the average and below average readers in their preference for excitement books, and that the percentage of second year children appreciating "excitement" showed a great increase over that for first years, most other categories having reduced percentages.'

When children were asked to state the type of books preferred, the conclusions were that:
> 'while the preference for adventure/mystery books heads the list for first and second year juniors, it shows a dramatic increase among the older age group ..... the preference for

Table 6.1 *Main preferred categories of books: whole sample*

Main categories preferred	Whole sample %
Funny stories	37.5
Mysteries	37
Ghost/horror	37
Adventure	37
Stories about teenagers	32
School stories	24
Science fiction	22.5
Love stories	22
TV stories	19
Animal/pet	15
Magic	14
Famous people	11
War — fiction	10
Historical — fiction	10
Sport — fiction	8
Art/craft books	8
'Factual' books	7.5
Other categories	5

N = 480

(Respondents were allowed to list up to four categories.)

amusing books, although it doesn't head this list, in general remains stable. However there is an increase with age in the preferences of below average readers and a decrease in preferences of above average readers, for amusing books. The reason for this is not evident but one might speculate that humorous stories may be easier to understand than the plot or theme of books of adventure'.

*Table 6.2   What kind of books would you like us to have more of?
Answers: whole sample*

Categories of books	Whole sample %
Adventure stories	13
Mystery stories	13
Teenage stories	12.5
Ghost/horror stories	12.5
Funny stories	8
School stories	7
Love stories	7
Science fiction	9
Hobbies/special interests	5
Magic fantasy stories	5
Biography/famous people	4
Animal stories	4.5
Art/craft	4
History	3.5
Science	3.5
'Vehicles' — space, car, bikes, planes, ship etc.	3
Supernatural stories	3
Other countries	3
Teach me/know how books	3
Comics	3
Sport stories, books for school subjects	3
Sport, non-fiction	3

N = 480

NB Categories were small because responses were voluntary and most children only answered one or two, though no limit was imposed.

In fact they were particularly interested in the difference between the children's stated preferences for adventure as opposed to their actual preference for funny stories and pursued this point further, concluding finally that:

'it appeared that the book chosen as most enjoyable by the children was more often an amusing book and less often an adventure book than might be expected from their stated general preferences. This was true for all levels of reading ability but more particularly for the average and above average readers and more particularly for boys. As so many children expressed enjoyment of amusing or funny books, is there a good supply of such books in both class and school libraries?'.

(It might be pertinent to add, is a good supply of such books published?)

6.1.1 Book preferences and age, sex, scheme membership

Sex in particular, and age of the children was far more significant in affecting book preferences than scheme use, although scheme users were more likely to mention 'funny stories' than non-users, who in turn were more likely to mention mysteries (see Table 6.3).

Differences between scheme users and non-users tended to disappear when stratified by sex, although it was interesting to note that war stories appeared to be the one category that was affected by scheme use. Among non-scheme users, 24% of the boys mentioned this as a preferred category, while no girls mentioned it at all. However, among scheme users, 6% of girls and only 17% of boys mentioned it. 'War' stories are to be found on the scheme and were chosen occasionally by the girls (see Chapter Five, Case studies of scheme users). Numbers involved are small but this could be an instance where deliberate 'exposure' to an unfamiliar type of book has effected change.

In general, there were clear lines of demarcation between boys' and girls' stated preferences, although funny stories, ghost/horror, mysteries and adventure stories transcended these lines (see Table 6.3). The case studies indicated very clearly that the children were very conscious of what constituted a 'boys' book, and a 'girls' book. The DES[14] noted that:

'there was a tendency for boys to dislike subject matter they associated with girls, and for all to dislike serious, sad or disturbing subject matter, girls rather more than boys ..... in pupil tastes in types of reading matter differences between boys and girls emerged strongly'.

Table 6.3 *Most popular book categories: boys/girls, scheme users/non-users*

Boys N = 168	%	Girls N = 307	%
Science fiction	47	Teenage stories	44
Adventure stories	44	Funny stories	39
Mystery stories	42	Ghost/horror stories	37
Ghost/horror stories	39	Mystery stories	34
Funny stories	34	Adventure stories	34
War stories	20	Love stories	33
TV stories	17.5	School stories	32
Sport stories	15	TV stories	20
Magic/fantasy stories	15	Animal stories	19
Factual	13	Famous people	11
Famous people	12	Art or craft	8
Scheme users N = 312	%	Non-users N = 168	%
Funny stories	40	Mystery stories	40
Adventure stories	39	Ghost/horror stories	36
Ghost/horror stories	38	Adventure stories	33
Mystery stories	36	Funny stories	31
Teenage stories	34	Teenage stories	28
School stories	25	Animal stories	26
Love stories	21	Love stories	25
Science fiction	21	School stories	20
TV stories	21	TV stories	17
Animal stories	12	Magic/fantasy stories	15

In particular, the girls showed far greater interest than the boys in 'books about teenagers like yourself' (see Tables 6.3 and 6.5). This was the most popular category for the girls, 44% mentioning it, as opposed to only 10% of the boys, who favoured science fiction most of all.

In fact, this difference probably masks a very similar interest in 'real-life situations', but expressed differently. The girls were inclined to be far more pragmatic as to what constituted 'real life'.

Table 6.4 Most popular book categories: age groups

11 years olds N = 141	%	12 years olds N = 143	%
Funny stories	52	Ghost/horror stories	39
Ghost/horror stories	45	Adventure stories	39
Adventure stories	45	Mystery stories	37
Mystery stories	45	Funny stories	36
Animal stories	24	Teenage stories	34
Science fiction	24	School stories	26
School stories	22	Love stories	22
Magic/fantasy stories	22	Science fiction	20
TV stories	19	TV stories	18
		Animal stories	17
13 year olds N = 93	%	14-18 year olds N = 93	%
Teenage stories	43	Teenage stories	49
Mystery stories	36	Mystery stories	32
Ghost/horror stories	33	Ghost/horror stories	30
Adventure stories	32	Adventure stories	29
Funny stories	29	Funny stories	29
Love stories	28	School stories	28
Science fiction	26	TV stories	24
School stories	23	Science fiction	24
War stories	17	Love stories	18
TV stories	17	Historical stories	15

This was clear from the reviews used in the case studies, where girls often disapproved of violence or other anti-social behaviour, on the grounds that it wasn't a proper way to behave and therefore was not very true to life. The boys on the other hand were able to regard fairly violent stories, for example teenage gang warfare in the United States, as perfectly 'real', presumably because the dilemmas facing the characters were accepted as real, even if the situation was unfamiliar. Thus to the girls, stories about youngsters in reasonably similar situations to their own were most 'real', and typical comments in answer to the question 'what would you like us to have more of?', included:

'divorces — something true'

'books about the problems you have'

'adventures about teenagers showing things that could really

*Table 6.5   What kind of books would you like us to have more of?
Answers: boys/girls, scheme users/non-users*

Boys N = 168	%	Girls N = 307	%
Science fiction	20	Teenage stories	18
Adventure stories	15	Adventure stories	12
Ghost/horror stories	13	Mystery stories	11
Mystery stories	12.5	Ghost/horror stories	11
Funny stories	9	Love stories	10.5
'Vehicles'	9	Funny stories	9
Scheme users N = 312	%	Non-users N = 168	%
Teenage stories (nearly all girls)	26	Adventure stories	18
Mystery stories	19	Ghost/horror stories	13
Ghost/horror stories	16	Mystery stories	11
Science fiction (nearly all boys)	11	Funny stories	8
Funny stories	11	Love stories	8
Adventure stories	11	'Vehicles'	8
Love stories (all girls)	11		

happen'
'things that happen in real life, not made up'.

For the boys, interest in 'reality' was expressed in preferences for sport, war, 'historical' and non-fiction generally (see Section 6.2). It was also said in passing by a 17 year old boy that his interest in science fiction was in no way incompatible with his preference for 'real-life things' because 'science fiction today was science fact tomorrow'.

It may be noted that the DES was:
'interested that (of the children who specifically outlined the subject matter or plot they wished more books would contain) a quarter expressed their preference for true situations, real facts or books that don't mislead'.

Apart from the categories already discussed, the girls liked love, school and animal stories while the boys liked war, sport and magic. There was also a tendency for the girls to be more aware of particular authors — or at least to name them — than the boys. Of the children mentioning fiction categories as being the kind of books

Table 6.6   What kind of books would you like us to have more of? Answers: age groups

11 years olds N = 141	%	12 years olds N = 143	%
Ghost/horror stories	18	Teenage stories	16
Funny stories	17	Adventure stories	12
Adventure stories	16	Ghost/horror stories	11
Mystery stories	14	Love stories	11
Science fiction	12	Mystery stories	9
Magic/fantasy stories	11	Science fiction	9
13 year olds N = 93	%	14-18 year olds N = 93	%
Teenage stories	16	Teenage stories	13
Mystery stories	15	Mystery stories	11
Adventure stories	15	Adventure stories	10
Funny stories	11	Art/craft	10
Ghost/horror stories	11	Love stories	8

they would like to see more of, 20%, mostly girls, named authors, of whom the most popular were Judy Blume and Enid Blyton.

There were few significant differences between age groups (see Tables 6.4 and 6.6) except that the younger readers showed a marked preference for funny stories and lack of interest in books about teenagers like themselves. Mysteries, adventure, ghost and horror held their interest for all the age groups analysed. (Because of small cell numbers, 14+ was used as an age category.)

6.2 Fiction/non-fiction

This project was concentrated on fiction reading, primarily because its focus was the reading schemes which do not include non-fiction. There were only two non-fiction categories amongst the 18 possible types of books suggested to the children, both very general categories, although a third category 'stories about famous people' was later designated as non-fiction.

In view of the fact therefore that the question, as to what type of books were preferred did undoubtedly direct the children towards fiction, it is perhaps noteworthy that a quarter of the children indicated preference for a non-fiction category as well as a fiction category, although responses to these categories were low compared to fiction categories (see Tables 6.1).

In terms of responses to the open-ended question, "what kind of books would you like us to have more of?", non-fiction figured more prominently, with greater differences between boys and girls emerging (see Table 6.7). Fifty-three percent of the boys mentioned fiction categories only, while 70% of the girls did so. On the other hand, 30% of the boys mentioned non-fiction only, as opposed to 18% of the girls.

Boys' preference for non-fiction starts early and is commented on by by most researchers.
'Boys showed a greater preference for "information" books than did girls ..... This particular finding has of course often been noted in previous investigations.'[15]
'When the statements faced a choice between stories and non-fiction, significantly more boys expressed a preference for non-fiction.'[16]

On the other hand it would appear to be wrong to assume from this

that boys are not interested in fiction per se — the DES concluded that:
'the great majority of the total sample (94%) enjoyed reading stories'.
Brenda Jones[2], in her study of 11-14 year olds, came to the conclusion that:
'the most popular type of book borrowed from both school and public library is the story book ..... whatever the ability of the child the story book is all important'.

The impression gained from the case studies was that while the boys were able to enjoy reading fiction if it was put in front of them many of them did not normally choose to do so, some of them apparently reading virtually no fiction at all, at least voluntarily.

Table 6.7   Indicated preferences for fiction and non-fiction: boys/girls

	Girls %	Boys %
Non-fiction categories only	18	30
Fiction only	70	53
Fiction and non-fiction categories	10	14
No stated preference	2	3
	N=307	N=168

7 Factors in choosing books

7.1 Effective choice

The Southgate Report[17] made a very crucial observation:
'It is not only the intention of teaching reading simply to produce children who *can* read, it should be the ultimate intention
to produce children who *do* read.'
The move from being a child who can read to a child who does voluntarily read is not an automatic one. Educational theory has long
been concerned about how to 'extend' children's reading in this way,
and is increasingly concerned with how to help and encourage children to make this move forward. It seems likely that developing the
ability to be able to choose enjoyable books — in other words exercise effective choice of books — is very important in this process.

To an extent, the role of the children's public library has always
been complementary to this, in terms of providing as pleasant and
helpful a place as possible for the child to be able to develop this
critical facility.

But many librarians — and teachers — now realize that the role of
the librarian in helping to promote effective choice is not nearly as
passive as perhaps imagined. It requires not only the ability to provide books that children are going to enjoy, which is no mean feat in
itself, but also the ability actively to guide the children, when necessary, and in ways they want, and can benefit from. The length of the
transition period, from a passive to active reader, when it occurs,
and also the amount of guidance that the child wants or needs, must
vary enormously from child to child. With all possible factors
pulling positively together, perhaps some children virtually jump
this stage in one go, almost as soon as they can read independently,
but for many children it is a much slower process and some children,
perhaps many, undoubtedly never complete it.

It should be emphasized that even the scheme users, who must be a
more literate than average group for their age, wanted and enjoyed
the kind of guidance exemplified by the schemes. They enjoyed
having a set list and even those children who wanted the list made
bigger, did not want total free choice. They particularly enjoyed
being able to use adults as a sounding board — adults who were not
'marking' them in any sense.

They were also equally certain that they did not want choice imposed on them, there was noticeably little enthusiasm for any set books read at school.

Children need to develop confidence in their ability to choose a book they are going to enjoy, confidence that for most of them will only come about when successful choices have been made. Furthermore, for most children, successful choices are only going to be made reasonably frequently, if careful, albeit unobtrusive, thought has been given to the kind of help or guidance they require, like and will benefit from most.

It does seem therefore that it is important to try to understand exactly how children choose fiction books, which factors are important to them and why, in order to know how best to help them choose.

Factors in choice fall very broadly into two groups: those relating to the book, and those relating to the child. It would be dangerous to make any sweeping assumptions as to the significance of either of these two broad areas.

For example, in 1975, a survey of top year primary school pupils in six schools[18] concluded that:
> 'the evidence relating to the books was stronger than the evidence relating to social class, library provisions (and reading ability)'.

This study looked at the school library books that were rejected — returned unread — by 200 children. They considered various factors, including sex, social class, reading ability, size of school library, and concluded that the most significant factors were length of book and degree of illustration. They concluded that:
> 'this might be seen to support Whitehead's contention that the attitudes of children towards books are influenced not so much by factors relating to the children themselves and the conditions under which they read, as they are by the factors inherent in the books'.

The authors of this report also noted that:
> 'time seemed to be an important factor for the children. The majority of books that were completed were those which were read within a few days',

and it was suggested that this might be one of the reasons why short books were so popular.

70

It may also be said that several of the apparently less avid readers on the scheme made a point of saying that feeling obliged to read a book all the way through, in a fairly short space of time, was much more interesting and beneficial than following their usual practice of reading books in bits and pieces, often not finishing them.

The project team concentrated primarily on factors inherent in the books, particularly as the sample involved was drawn exclusively from library users and not from the general population. All the children were asked what were the most important factors in choosing a fiction book, and this was the primary focus of interest throughout the in-depth interviews with scheme users.

7.2   Content of the books

Most of the children seemed to have quite clear ideas as to the types of fiction books they liked — and disliked — and also as to the type of books they felt would be liked by the opposite sex (see Chapter 6). Of course children do have broad preferences, but there is evidence to suggest that boundaries of preferred fiction categories are not actually as fixed as one might imagine from the positiveness of the children's responses. For example, although girls and boys did show some clear preferences for some categories of books (see Table 6.3), a humorous story, a fast-moving story or a story that seems to be 'real', could transcend many subject barriers.

Many surveys have indicated that extent to which funny stories are enjoyed, by children of all ages (see Chapter 6) and also that adventure and mystery runs a fairly close second. Along with ghost/horror stories, these were the four most popular categories among the 11+ readers as well (see Table 6.1).

Of all the items suggested to the children as possibly being important in helping them choose a book, the two clear favourites were that it should be a good story and that the book should seem interesting (see Table 7.1).

Of course not many children were expected actually to disagree with either of these statements, they were included primarily to ensure that all the children had at least some items they could agree with without requiring too much thought, but it was interesting to note the clear lead that these items had, and also of course to delve into exactly what was meant by 'good' or 'interesting'.

Table 7.1 Important aspects of choosing a book: whole sample

Aspect	%
A good story	92
Book seems interesting	89
Reading the blurb	80
Good titles	76
Recommendations	66
Good picture on the front	58
Knowing about the book	47
The writer	42
Enough illustrations	39
Book not too short	37
Print not too small	36
Book not too long	33
Seeing story on TV	29
Paperback	28

N = 480

There was little doubt that a 'good' story was almost invariably a fast-moving, and easily understandable one. Several children specifically mentioned that they looked for long descriptive passages in books and if they found them, they knew it *was not* going to be a good book, because it was going to be boring, e.g. slow moving. Perhaps the ability to appreciate characterization and atmosphere is something that only comes with maturity. It certainly was not appreciated by the sample, and they did not seem noticeably less than averagely mature for their age groups. It was noticeable that even the older children disliked books that did not have a 'proper' story with a clearly defined start and finish. They did not like distractions from the plot, such as dialects or chronological jumping about.

The other main characteristic required of a good story seemed to be that it should be 'real' in some sense, and this is perhaps related to the need to be able to make sense of the book as a whole.

The girls and boys tended to have slightly different interpretations of 'reality' (see Chapter 6), the main difference appearing to be that, for the girls, reality centred around people, whereas for the boys, reality centred around things or events. Thus, apart from the four most popular categories already mentioned, the girls said they preferred stories about teenagers like themselves, love stories and school stories, while the boys expressed preference for science fiction, and war stories, and also for non-fiction generally (see Table 6.7).

They were united in reserving their strongest criticism for books portraying lifestyles that struck them as meaningless or silly. A boring book was one where the plot moved slowly but a 'terrible' book was one that was 'unreal' and therefore just plain silly or even ridiculous. Indeed several children expressed polite amazement at the fact that the authors had bothered to write what they regarded as being patently 'bad' books.

Given that it was important for the book to be 'interesting', most of the children in this sample had devised methods of assessing this, firstly involving how to pick out a book initially, and secondly, how to assess its subject content, its readability and whether or not it was going to be 'good'.

7.3 The process of selecting fiction

The first stage in this process is to identify the part of the library that books are going to be chosen from. Library organization of fiction bookstock was not a concern of this project, partly because considerable thought has already been given to this particular aspect of children's librarianship by most public library authorities. (This might not apply to school libraries which do not have the benefit of a qualified librarian.) It was however noted that the greatest categories of responses to the question 'what would make the library better for you', were in terms of improving guiding and access to books, and this was from a group that were almost entirely regular library users.

It was also noticeable that the girls seemed to be far more adept than the boys at working through the whole process of sorting out a good book — one wonders how this is related to the fact that girls read more fiction than boys — which came first?

Having identified the part of the library from which books will be chosen, the next stage is to select some books for further investigation. If this implies that the process of choice can be fairly lengthy, this is indeed the impression received. Perhaps this is why the reading schemes are so popular with children who already read: not only do the schemes enable them to jump the initial stages in the process, by presenting the child with a ready made selection of 'possibles', they also offer considerable help in the whole process of choice by having an adult available who is able and willing to describe the book.

Title or cover are the things that catch most of the children's eyes initially, although the girls were slightly more likely to look out for particular authors, or series, and there was some evidence that the older children had begun to care that the books should look — or be — new. Cover was said by several children to be important because, hopefully, it gave them a clue as to the subject matter of the book. If it was a non-committal cover, particularly if it was just words, it had little informative value and was unlikely to be noticed.

Paperbacks as such were not regarded as being very important by the majority of the sample, although one of the characteristics usually associated with paperbacks — a good picture on the front — was important. It may be that lack of interest in paperbacks is related to when and where books are read, insofar as one of the main advantages of paperbacks is that they are light and easy to carry. For example, the DES[19] found that most 11 year olds preferred to read their books in quiet places, at home in their bedroom and particularly, in bed. As one young library user pointed out, paperbacks are difficult to read in bed because they do not stay flat! It may also be that many of the young children's hardback and paperback fiction editions are not nearly as physically distinct in their format and appearance as adult fiction.

Recommendation, or knowing about the book in some way, was important to many children. The effect of television programmes or films in stimulating interest is a widely observed phenomenon, although there is not necessarily a direct relationship between seeing a story and enjoying reading it, if only because the books,

Table 7.2   Important aspects of choosing a book: boys/girls

Important aspects: boys	%	Important aspects: girls	%
Good story	94	Good story	91
Book interesting	91	Book interesting	89
Good title	75	Reading blurb	85
Blurb	74	Good titles	77
Recommended	61	Recommended	63
Good pictures	56	Good pictures	60
Knowing about the book	51	The writer	45
Enough illustrations	46	Knowing about the book	45
Book not too short	38	Book not too short	36
The writer	37	Enough illustrations	36
Print not too small	35	Print not too small	36
Book not too long	34	Book not too long	33
Seeing story on TV	29	Story on TV	30
Paperbacks	25	Paperbacks	30

N=168   N=307

which are often classics in their way, are often too difficult for many children to actually enjoy reading. Three-quarters of the sample said that recommendations were important to them, usually meaning recommendations from friends. There was noticeably less enthusiasm for recommendations from teachers, whose motives tended to be regarded as potentially suspect!

Having made a tentative choice, the next stage in the process was usually reading a part of the book. Eighty percent of the sample said they read the 'blurb' which was interpreted fairly liberally to

Table 7.3 Important aspects of choosing a book: scheme users/non-users

Important aspects Scheme users	%	Important aspects Non-users	%
Good story	90	Good story	95
Book interesting	88	Book interesting	92
Blurb	85	Good titles	78
Good titles	76	Blurb	73
Good pictures on front	61	Recommendations	66
Recommendations	60	Pictures on front	55
The author	44	Knowing about the book	55
Knowing about the book	43	Enough illustrations	47
Book not too short	37	Book not too long	40
Print not too small	36	The author	39
Enough illustrations	35	Book not too short	36
Book not too long	30	Print not too small	34
Paperbacks	29	Story on TV	31
Seeing story on TV	28	Paperbacks	28

N=312   N=168

mean any part of the cover or inside pages, and often meant in fact reading some of the actual text. The first page, or a randomly selected page was often read to check on 'style' — words not too difficult, no obviously boring bits — as well as content. The girls appeared to be more likely to assess the books quite methodically, looking at chapter headings and so on. There were indications that the older children looked for further clues as to the books' probable 'value', e.g. information about the author, quotes from reviewers or

Table 7.4 Important aspects of choosing a book: age groups

Aspect	Age groups %			
	11	12	13	14+
Print not too small	49	29	37	33
Book not too long	33	29	36	34
Enough illustrations	44	42	33	32
Good pictures	58	60	56	58
Good titles	80	75	72	77
Blurb	73	86	85	80
Knowing about the book	48	41	48	55
Seeing story on TV	31	33	25	22
Book seems interesting	88	92	87	90
Book not too short	41	33	29	39
The writer	41	45	42	39
Paperback	23	36	48	30
A good story	90	94	88	91
Recommendations	62	61	56	69

N=141 N=143 N=93 N=93

mention of awards, whether many people had borrowed it, when it was published, and so on.

Length of book, size of print and degree of illustration were less important factors to the sample although it may still be noted that nearly 40% of the children said that 'enough illustration' was important to them. It was said that illustrations help to fix a scene in the mind of the reader. Fenwick[20] suggested that a book with less than 5% content devoted to illustration was unlikely to be popular, and noted that popular books for their 10 and 11 year olds tended to have between 10% and 20% devoted to illustration. They also noted that there was:

'little doubt that children fight shy of lengthy books'.

They suggested 40,000 words as an upper limit for popular books, and were somewhat dismayed to find that,

'an examination of the school libraries (concerned) showed that they contained a considerable number of books of 65,000 words or more'.

Amongst the sample, there were some differences between scheme users and non-users concerning length of book and degree of illustration (see Table 7.3) scheme users being generally less concerned with either.

Readability of a book is obviously important insofar as there are boundaries to most children's reading ability, and if they do inadvertently choose a book that lies outside this boundary, it is unlikely to be read. However, being within the boundaries of the child's reading ability is by no means enough to ensure that it is going to be actually read. Fenwick[21] tested the hypothesis that children with a lower than average reading ability would be more likely to return library books unread, but found this unproven by their results: there was no difference in book rejection between lower, average, or above average readers. The DES[22] noted that in terms of responses to the questions to:

'elicit information about children's criteria for likes and dislikes, ... the preoccupations that emerged were principally to do with content and effect, cost and format. Preoccupation with difficulty was rarely overtly expressed, although responses to do with format could be interpreted as implicit comments on difficulty level'.

Of course 'readability' is not simply a matter of decipherable words. For many children it was obviously important that the book should make sense as a whole. It was apparent from the in-depth interviews that one of the indirect benefits of many aspects of the scheme was in helping the children to make sense of what they were reading. Feeling obliged to read the books through carefully, in a fairly short space of time, talking about them and writing about them, were all perceived by the scheme users themselves as having the end result of making the books far more interesting.

7.4   Sources of reading materials: schools and public libraries

The children in the sample were asked where they got their fiction reading books from, other than the public library they were using (see Table 7.5). This was not an area pursued in depth by the project, but it is interesting to note that the school library was a significant source of books for many of the children.

Table 7.5   Sources of story books, other than public libraries: whole sample, age groups

Sources	Whole sample %	11 %	12 %	13 %	14+ %
School library	69	63	81	73	68
Bought	54	55	57	52	61
Parents	25	33	27	21	21
Friends	23	17	18	27	38
Other relatives	20	27	19	19	17
Another library	20	23	20	18	22

N=141 N=143 N=93   N=93

Brenda Jones, in 1974,[23] had concluded that:
'children of the 11 to 14 age range largely depend on the school library for books they require and the public library should be catering for recreational reading needs and providing books of a practical nature'.
But the evidence from this enquiry shows that for some children at least, school libraries are a source of recreational reading as well, and it seems quite likely that for many children — those who never use public libraries — they may be the main, or only source of recreational reading.

Insofar as educational theory continues to emphasize 'the importance of each child learning to appreciate how enjoyable and useful reading is'[24], the role of the school library in provision of recreational reading is increasingly being recognized, and promoted by teachers.

It is a fact that two-thirds of the children on Westminster's reading schemes came from voluntary aided or private schools, also that all the most avid readers in an admittedly very small sub-sample of scheme users came from such schools. This is not inherently surprising, given the distribution of schools in Westminster. There are more voluntary aided secondary schools in Westminster than there are 'county' schools and although the three county schools have a combined school roll that is greater than the voluntary aided secondary schools, they are all situated on the edges of the borough and undoubtedly draw many of their children from outside Westminster. Nevertheless, it would be a very sad case of wasted resources to see the growing overlapping of the roles of school and public libraries unaccompanied by a growing awareness of the value of close relationships between teachers and librarians.

The DES[25] has recently commented that:
'the crux of reading is the independent use made of reading skills by pupils, both in the short and long term'.
Both teachers and librarians have important roles to play in fostering such independent use.

8   Chapter summaries

Chapter 1

During the school summer holidays, Westminster's Children's Libraries operate graded holiday reading schemes, open to all children, in their eight main junior libraries.

This report is an account of a survey, carried out during summer 1981, of 312 children enrolled in these schemes and a further 168 library users not enrolled in schemes. The survey was confined to children aged between 11 and 18. Certain other relevant surveys have also been extensively referred to in chapter discussions.

Various sources of information were utilized, the main ones being formal questionnaires, informal tape-recorded interviews with children, and some reviews written by the children. It is hoped that the information and ideas put forward in this report will provide insights into and stimulate interest in the reading habits of the 11+ age group and that it will provide some useful avenues to pursue for those concerned with producing, promoting or providing books for young urban teenagers.

Chapter 2

In the sample of summer junior library users over 11, 80% were aged between 11 and 14, with very few over 15. Approximately two-thirds were girls, one-third boys, with the girls slightly more likely to be older than the boys. Scheme users were more likely to be a little younger than scheme non-users. The peak age for scheme use was 11, among scheme non-users it was 12. It was noted that girls, on average, read more fiction than boys, and also that interest in reading is said to peak at around the age of 11. Allowing for the fact that more girls than boys use the library, slightly more girls were attracted to the schemes than boys.

The great majority of the children lived very near to their library and had lived in London for over five years. Only three percent had lived in London for less than one year. Scheme users were marginally more likely to be longer term residents than non-users. Forty-six percent of the children were judged to belong to specified ethnic minority groups. There was little difference between ethnic backgrounds of children enrolled in schemes or not enrolled, though it was noted that Spanish (and European children generally) were under-represented on the scheme and in the libraries. Thirty percent of the children spoke a language other than English at home, though English was the preferred home language for half of these. Thirteen percent of the sample read in a language other than English, noticeably Spanish, excluding languages learnt routinely as part of school curriculum.

Most of the children were members of Westminster's children's libraries. Scheme users were slightly more likely to be members than non-users.

Three-quarters of the sample were regular library users. Once again, scheme users were slightly more likely to be regular library users than scheme non-users.

A majority of the children said that neither of their parents were public library members, 61% of scheme non-users, 54% of scheme users.

Chapter 3

Most of the children did not feel that too many books in the library were too hard, or too long, or that they did not understand how the books were arranged.

A majority also did not feel that too many books were all words, although 40% did agree with this statement. Boys were more likely to agree with this than girls, also the younger children. Amongst 11 year olds, 51% agreed.

An earlier survey of 10 and 11 year olds found:
'a significant relationship between book rejection and the number of words and proportion of illustration which a book contained'.

A majority of children agreed that it was difficult to choose a book from all those on the shelves. This proportion did not vary signifi-cantly with age, scheme use, or sex. The recent DES report on 11 year olds[25] found that:
'over half the sample experienced difficulty in locating suitable

books in libraries'.

The children were asked to suggest any ways in which the library could be improved. The largest single category of answers involved greater guidance, but via indirect rather than direct help, such as classification and cataloguing systems, displays, shelf guidance and so on.

The second main group of answers was concerned with activities. Not surprisingly, there was interest in activities particularly designed for older junior library users. Suggestions included author displays, talking about books, having reading schemes more often and librarian-for-a-day schemes.

Many other suggestions and ideas were put forward by the children.

Chapter 4

More children heard about the reading schemes from their libraries than from any other source, and most children in this age group have used the schemes one or more times before.

Of all age groups using the schemes, 40% drop out before completing. More evidence is needed to ascertain how far this is deliberate dropping out, or just inadvertent failure to complete in time.

In general, the sample appeared to be happy with the particular schemes they had selected although a tendency to regard the minimum age for entry to Bookmaster as an unspoken maximum age for entry to Bookworm was observed, a tendency that could be unhelpful to some children. The precise terminology used by the librarians when introducing and describing the schemes can be very influential.

The best liked aspect of the schemes was said to be having something to do in the holidays, particularly amongst the girls. It became apparent at later stages in the project, that feeling obliged to read a book through thoroughly and having the chance to express views about it — without fear of being 'marked' or assessed in any way — were important aspects of the scheme. They made the reading of the books far more enjoyable and rewarding. Many of the case study children, particularly the older ones, made a point of emphasizing the fact that the schemes were, to them, a more enjoyable way of passing their time than any of the alternatives available to them including adventure playgrounds, playcentres and so on.

Where criticism of the schemes was offered, it was largely in terms of wanting a larger set list of books.

Chapter 5

Twenty case studies were drawn up, 10 of which have been presented in this report. The case studies were based on dossiers consisting of formal questionnaires, informal interviews and book reviews written by the children. The case study approach does not lend itself to formal content summary but as a methodology it was very successful in allowing comments, ideas and preferences already noted to be probed further.

Chapter 6

In the sample as a whole, the best liked categories of fiction were funny stories, mysteries, adventure stories, ghost and horror stories.

Apart from these four favourites, boys and girls indicated clear preferences, girls for books about teenagers like themselves and boys for science fiction. Both sexes had a clear liking for a fast moving plot and 'reality' in stories.

Boys, as expected, indicated stronger preference for non-fiction than girls.

Chapter 7

Many educationalists have noted that, in the context of reading:
'of concern is not just the question whether pupils can read, but whether they do and will read. Of particular concern ..... are pupils who have the ability to read books but choose not to do so'.[26]
It is suggested that confidence in the ability to select an enjoyable book from library shelves is a factor in whether children 'choose' voluntarily to read or not, and also that such confidence can be

actively encouraged, firstly by judicious selection and organization of bookstock and secondly by paying greater attention to the process of choice undertaken by most children and the forms of guidance they seem to want and benefit from. Most librarians have already given considerable thought to the former and are actively interested in the latter.

Selection of enjoyable books — the process of effective choice — is not an easy one, and there was some evidence to suggest that it gets harder as the children get older. Girls seemed generally to be rather more adept at the whole process than the boys — is this why they read more fiction, or is it because they read more fiction?

In terms of the way in which books are selected, visual clues to subject matter, such as cover and illustration (in the absence of fiction categories or age groupings) were important even to this sample of largely regular library users. Recommendations from others were also important, provided that the 'others' were perceived to be in tune with the child's wavelength. Friends particularly qualified for this, teachers mostly did not although it was noted that school libraries are almost certainly a significant source of recreational reading for most school age children, and were an important source for the sample.

Finally, the chance to express, and discuss views with an adult — a key feature of the schemes — was noted as being particularly valued by the children, often apparently compensating for having read books that had been actively disliked. The DES[27] noted that:
'talking about books was by far the most popular activity as a follow-up to reading'.
This was true of this group, with the proviso that there should be no element of assessment in the talking (or writing) about the books.

It seems likely that the roles of the school and junior public library are increasingly overlapping. Both are concerned with promoting 'independent use made of reading skills' and a strong case can be made for mutually advantageous co-operation between teachers and librarians towards a common end: the utilization of existing skills and expertise to make the selection of enjoyable fiction in libraries by children easier and more effective.

9 Conclusions and recommendations

9.1 Conclusions

'Conclusions' is a largely inappropriate term for an investigative survey. The chapter summaries outline the project's substantive findings. These can be related here to the project aims, which were:

(a) to explore book preferences of young people aged between 11 and 18;

(b) to collect basic data on the use, attraction and observable effects of the reading scheme;

(c) to explore certain aspects of library use.

Book preferences, and certain aspects of library use, and users, have been explored (see Chapters 2, 3 and 6). It should be remembered that the book preferences relate to a sample of library users, primarily aged between 11 and 14. The schemes are used by the majority of summer library users, and there are few significant differences between the children who enrol on the schemes and those who don't.

The major attractions of the schemes are the personal involvement of the librarians, the chance for self-expression for the children and the fact that the books on the set lists are thought to be enjoyable. It is also important to many of the older children that the scheme should sufficiently occupy their time. The attraction of the various scheme incentives is, as one would expect, stronger to the younger readers, and apparently to the boys.

The schemes have the effect of persuading many children to read more books, or to read books more thoroughly than they would otherwise have done, and also to enjoy the experience of reading books more than they would have done on their own. The schemes also give the less experienced library users practice in choosing books for themselves and the more experienced users guidance toward books they might have otherwise missed.

Some children, mainly the older ones and more probably the girls, can be persuaded to widen their range of reading interests apart from being introduced to new authors within their usual range, though this is resisted by a lot of children, particularly the less avid readers.

The schemes are probably least effective — or have least effect — on the children over 11 who have not developed the habit of independent fiction reading. It may be that these children are finding that even the top list of Bookworm, i.e. the Bookwizard list, is too demanding in terms of degree of time and concentration required to be spent on an activity that doesn't greatly attract them, or is perhaps difficult for them to cope with, but yet feel unable to participate in anything 'lower' than Bookwizard or even Bookmaster.

The effect of the schemes on the librarians — and the libraries — should also be noted. The librarians learn a great deal about children's reading, their library users, and their users' preferences for types of books. In the long run, this must be of enormous benefit, both to their relationship with current and future users, and to the enjoyment value of their fiction bookstock. At the same time, the children gain considerable confidence in use of books, the library, and the librarians. This must also be of mutual benefit.

In the light of the project's substantive findings, and these broad 'conclusions', the following recommendations are put forward for discussion.

9.2 Recommendations

1   Further information is still needed on the 'missing' children in the sample. Where are the children over 14? If use of the junior library drops off dramatically by 14, do these children simply stop using public libraries? Are they in the adult library? Do they try the adult library? Were they only junior library users by virtue of school class visits? This is an avenue that would be very useful to pursue further, there is still very little known about this age group. A detailed look at young people using Westminster's adult libraries could be potentially very instructive and would hopefully complement this investigation.

Of the children enrolling in the reading schemes, 40% fail to complete. There were few significant differences between those enrolled on the schemes and those not enrolled, but it may be that the significant differences are between those who complete the schemes, and those who don't, particularly as the branch librarians do actively encourage as many users as possible to join the schemes. (This in itself is a valuable aspect of the scheme because it prevents only certain groups of children self-selecting themselves to enter the schemes.) It might prove to be useful to investigate further the 40% who don't complete, in order to determine how far it represents deliberate dropping out, due to disliked aspects of the scheme, and how far it is unintentional failure to complete in time. Given that a proportion of failure is undoubtedly unintentional, it is not suggested that this should be a major exercise.

2   The schemes are undoubtedly successful in achieving their primary aims of promoting enjoyment of reading, and keeping the children reading, for a majority of library users. The schemes attract users of all age groups, from two to 18, and over a wide ability range, though more so among the younger than older users. Many children use the schemes year after year.

The schemes also benefit the staff, who develop considerable knowledge and expertise concerning their users, and the books that their users enjoy. The major disadvantage to the staff, apart from the amount of work involved, which can be quite considerable, is the degree of interest and concentration required of them. It is no mean feat to move straight from a four year old to a 14 year old, or to demonstrate interest and enthusiasm in a book that has been discussed 20 times before and tribute should be paid to the librarians who not only do this, but do it well, and to the children's evident satisfaction. The rules on only one book a day, and no 'testing' after five o'clock were found to be necessary to make the load tolerable for the library staff!

Given the amount of effort that goes into the schemes, and the unique relationship that the librarians establish with their users, it may also be noted that far greater use should ideally be made of the information that routinely emerges each year. For example, the children's scheme registration forms can easily elicit information on which books are chosen most frequently, and annual lists of most popular — and best enjoyed — books for particular age groupings could be produced. These would surely be of considerable interest to everyone concerned with promoting the idea that reading is enjoyable, not least of all, teachers. The book reviews are also a very rich source of knowledge and further information concerning book likes, and dislikes, of particular age groups.

In response to existing demand for this kind of information, a brief report on the schemes, with a very general analysis of reviews of the books on the Bookmaster list is already produced annually.[28]

3   In view of the fact that one of ILEA's current interests is the under-achievement of girls, it may be that the self-imposed lines of demarcation between boys' and girls' reading, particularly the extent of non-fiction read, should be giving some cause for concern. It's difficult to persuade children to cross self-imposed boundaries, but it would be very valuable to look more closely at ways in which this could be done.

4   The fact that children have difficulty in finding enjoyable books in libraries should be recognized and acted on, in both school and public libraries, both of which are potentially important sources of recreational reading for children, and both of which share at least one common aim: the desire to move children through the stage of being a child who can read to the stage of being a child who does read.

Furthermore, it is wrong to assume that all children have completed this stage by the age of 11, and it would be valuable for continued thought to be given to the needs of the older children who are not able or experienced fiction readers, or library users.

References

1. Leng, I J (1968). *Children in the library*. Cardiff, University of Wales Press.
2. Jones, B (1978). *Children's use of libraries. Report of a survey carried out at Francis Combe Lower School, Abbots Langley, November 1974*. London, DES.
3. Department of Education & Science (1978). *The libraries' choice*. Library Advisory Council, Library Information Series No.10. London, HMSO.
4. Inner London Education Authority (1979). *Report on the 1978 census of those ILEA pupils for whom English was not a first language*. ILEA Report No.9484. London, ILEA.
5. *ibid*, p.8.
6. City of Westminster Development Plan (1978). *Population and housing*. Topic Paper T6. London, City of Westminster.
7. Jones, B (1978). *op. cit.*, p.6.
8. Fenwick, G (1975). Junior school pupils' rejection of school library books, *Educational Research*, 17(2), February 1975, pp.143-149.
9. Southgate, V (1981). *Extending beginning reading*. London, The Schools Council.
10. Department of Education & Science (1981). *Language performance in schools*. Primary survey. Report No.1. London Assessment of Performance Unit, HMSO.
11. Moser, C A (1971). *Survey methods in social investigation*. London, Heinemann.
12. Department of Education & Science (1981). *op. cit.*, Chapter 3: Attitudes to reading.
13. Southgate, V (1981). *op. cit.*, Chapter 14: Children's views on books.
14. Department of Education & Science (1981). *op. cit.*, Chapter 3
15. Southgate, V (1981). *op. cit.*, p.223.
16. Department of Education & Science (1981). *op. cit.*, p.81.
17. Southgate, V (1981). *op. cit.*, p.35.
18. Fenwick, G (1975). *op. cit.*, p.148.
19. Department of Education & Science (1981). *op. cit.*, Chapter 3.
20. Fenwick, G (1975). *op. cit.*, p.148.
21. *ibid*.
22. Department of Education & Science (1981). *op. cit.*, p.81
23. Jones, B (1978). *op. cit.*, p.7.
24. Department of Education & Science (1975). *A language for life* (The Bullock Report) London, HMSO.
25. Department of Education & Science (1981). *op. cit.*, p.53.
26. *ibid*. p.53.
27. *ibid*. p.81.
28. Roberts, L (1975-   ). *Annual reports on the Bookmaster scheme*. London, Westminster City Libraries.

Appendix 1 Westminster's reading scheme

1.1 Details of the scheme

During the school summer holidays, Westminster children's libraries operate a graded reading scheme (which is now really three overlapping schemes), open to anyone under 18. Pre-readers are not excluded: the books may be read to them by parents or other members of their family.

This account of the way the scheme has developed is a very brief introduction only for those unfamiliar with it. More specific and detailed information may be obtained from the head of the children's library service, Lorna Roberts, who produces documentation annually. In 1975, when it started, the scheme was called 'Bookworm'. The following is an extract from the 1979 Report on the scheme.

'From the beginning it was created to meet the particular needs of Westminster children, and over the years (the schemes) have changed to meet the children's changing needs. The objectives of the scheme are:

(a) to keep children reading throughout the long summer holiday;

(b) to encourage children to explore a wider range of author and styles;

(c) to take positive action to encourage and promote reading for pleasure and enjoyment.

The scheme was intended as a contribution towards encouraging reading in a community where many children had reading difficulties and needed positive help and motivation. The schemes operate in the eight main children's libraries for the six weeks of the summer holidays. New booklists are compiled each year, to cover all age groups. Books are carefully selected to appeal to children in an inner city area. The incentives and organization are reviewed each year.'

In 1975, Bookworm required each child to select, read and discuss with a librarian at least five books from their chosen list. When this task was completed, the children were deemed to have completed the scheme, although they were free to carry on reading and discussing as many books as they wanted. Attractive and colourful Bookworm 'trails' were prominently displayed in the libraries participating, featuring a series of numbered shapes (animals, witches, circles, etc) and as each child completed a book, they placed one of their name stickers on the appropriate shape. Badges and bookmarks were given out at the start, and certificates were given at the end for those who had completed the scheme. These certificates were formally presented at a special evening ceremony held in the branch libraries, to which visitors were invited.

The schemes have followed this basic pattern since then, though there are now three tiers to the scheme.

'By 1977, it was becoming obvious that so many of the points that were making Bookworm such a marvellous success for so many groups (like the less able reader, the enthusiastic beginner reader and the reluctant reader) were creating a major obstacle for the dedicated older reader. They spent a week carefully reading and enjoying their teenage novels, while younger brothers and sisters raced through a book each day. A new scheme was needed which would remove older children from the competition of young Bookworms. In 1978, Bookmaster was introduced.'

Bookmaster is open to 11 to 18 year olds. They must read at least four books and write a review of each book. If they complete this task they are awarded a certificate at a special — and rather grand — presentation ceremony attended by the Lord Mayor of Westminster and a celebrity author, whose books are included on the year's list. (In 1980 for example, the author was Roald Dahl, in 1981 it was Joan Aiken.) Extracts from the Bookmaster reviews are published annually, entitled *Our verdict,* and are distributed within the libraries.

'Bookmaster is intended for the able reader. The top list of Bookworm covers a reading age of nine to fifteen, and staff encourage young teenagers to choose the scheme they will feel happiest with.'

However, it became apparent, as time progressed, that a proportion of over-11s were enrolling in Bookmaster before they were ready to do so, largely because Bookworm came to be primarily used by eight to nine year olds, although of course not many of these children were necessarily using the top Bookworm list. Therefore this summer, 1981, a third category, Bookwizard, was introduced, using the top Bookworm list. To complete this, the children were required to read and discuss four books and write one review. This was promoted as a scheme for those who were 'too old' for Bookworm but who didn't want to do Bookmaster, without any formal age limits being attached.

One thousand four hundred and forty-seven children of all ages enrolled in Westminster's scheme this year. It is undoubtedly a very popular scheme among library users, and many of the children enrol year after year. Great care is taken to ensure that no child who really wants to complete their scheme fails to do so, and the children received as much encouragement, support, and active help as they appear to want or need, from the library staff.

1.2   Westminster Bookwizard: set list 1981

Author	*Title*
Ashley, Bernard	Break in the sun
Barber, Antonia	The amazing Mr Blunden
Bawden, Nina	Rebel on a rock
Blume, Judy	Otherwise known as Sheila the great
Breinburg, Petronella	One day, another day
Brown, Lindsay	The treasure of Dubarry Castle
Brown, Roy	Chips and the crossword gang
Byars, Betsy	The Pinballs
Chambers, Robin	Shadows in the pit
Cleary, Beverly	Henry and Ribsy
Cresswell, Helen	Bagthorpes unlimited
Dicks, Terrance	The case of the missing masterpiece
Eagar, Frances	Time tangle
Farmer, Penelope	Charlotte sometimes
Foster, John L	My friend Cheryl
Garner, Alan	Elidor
Grant, Gwen	Private — keep out
Guy, Rosa	The friends
Hardcastle, Michael	Soccer comes first
Hill, Douglas	Galactic warlord
Jones, Diana Wynne	Charmed life
Lavelle, Sheila	My best friend
Leeson, Robert	Harold and Bella, Jimmy and me
Lewis, C Day	The Otterbury incident
Mace, Elisabeth	The ghost diviners
Manning, Rosemary	The dragon's quest
Mark, Jan	Under the autumn garden
Needle, Jan	The size spies
Peterson, Barbara	Henny takes a hand

Pearce, Philippa	The battle of Bubble and Squeak
Rockwell, Thomas	How to eat fried worms
Salkey, Andrew	Hurricane
Storr, Catherine	Pen friends
Thompson, Howard	The battle of Billy's pond
Rowe Townsend, John	Gumble's yard
Wakefield, S A	Bottersnikes and Gumbles
Waterhouse, Keith and Hall, Willis	The trials of Worzel Gummidge
Welch, Ronald	Tank commander
White, E B	Charlotte's web
Williams, Ursula Moray	Bogwoppit

1.3   Westminster Bookmaster: set list 1981

Author	*Title*
Adams, Don	The hitch-hiker's guide to the galaxy
Aiken, Joan	Go saddle the sea
Aiken, Joan	A bundle of nerves
Amis, Kingsley	Lucky Jim
Austen, Jane	Sense and sensibility
Burnford, Sheila	The incredible journey
Carter, Peter	Under Goliath
Cate, Dick	One of the gang
Chambers, Aidan	World zero minus
Chetwynd-Hayes, R	The 10th Fontana book of great ghost stories
Christie, Agatha	The Seven Dials mystery
Collins, Wilkie	The moonstone
Cookson, Catherine	The Lord and Mary Ann
Darke, Marjorie	The first of midnight
Dillon, Eilis	The San Sebastian
Doubtfire, Dianne	Sky girl
Durrell, Lawrence	White eagles over Serbia
Fleming, Ian	Goldfinger
Foster, John	Watch all night
Golding, William	Lord of the flies
Greene, Graham	Brighton rock
Guareschi, Giovanni	Tales from the little world of Don Camillo
Hawes, Chris	Maybe I'm amazed
Hewitt, Jenny	Judy in love
Hentoff, Nat	This school is driving me crazy
Hines, Barry	Kes

Hinton, S E	Rumble fish
Hocken, Sheila	Emma and I
Hoyle, Fred	The black cloud
Kavanagh, P J	Scarf Jack
Keating, H R E	Filmi filmi Inspector Ghote
Leach, Christopher	A temporary open air life
Lee, Harper	To kill a mocking bird
Le Guin, Ursula	City of illusions
MacDonald, Shelagh	No end to yesterday
Marks, J M	Border kidnap
Marshall, James Vance	Walkabout
Mowat, Farley	The black joke
Naipaul, V S	Miguel Street
Needle, Jan	My mate Shofiq
Rees, David	The Exeter blitz
Salway, Vance	Second to the right and straight on till morning
Storr, Catherine	Who's Bill
Townsend, John Rowe	Noah's castle
Turgenev, I	First love
Van der Post, Laurens	Flaming feather
Waterhouse, Keith	Billy liar
Webster, Jean	Dady-long-legs
Welch, Ronald	Tank commander
Wells, H G	The history of Mr Polly
Westall, Robert	The wind eye
Wodehouse, P G	Summer moonshine
Wyndham, John	The day of the triffids
Zindel, Paul	My darling my hamburger

Appendix 2   Data collection

It was decided to employ two main methods of data collection. These were formal printed questionnaires and informal, semi-structured taped interviews. The book reviews written by some of the children were also analysed.

2.1   The questionnaires

The questionnaire was in two parts, the first part designed for all library users, the second part for scheme users only. The interviewing was carried out simultaneously in eight branches. All library users were sampled in a one-week period, scheme users were sampled throughout a seven-week period. All the junior library staff were involved in the interviewing. Piloting and interviewer training was a combined exercise. Fairly detailed 'notes for interviewers' were distributed and discussed at two briefing sessions attended by all junior library staff, in two groups. These notes covered project briefing, sampling method, interviewing, and so on. All staff were asked to pilot at least one questionnaire, still in draft form, and to write an assessment of the interview, and the draft questionnaire. Following analysis of everyone's assessment, and a further discussion session, the final versions of the two parts of the questionnaire were produced, with accompanying explanatory notes (see Appendix 3).

During the first week of the surveying a research worker visited all branches to discuss and iron out any minor problems/queries etc, and to check through the returned questionnaires for completeness. All questionnaires were signed by the staff member administering them. Using the entire staff as interviewers created certain problems. It was difficult to communicate with such a large body of 'field workers' and it was also difficult, at times, for the staff to be both librarians and research assistants, particularly as the reading schemes could be very labour intensive. The situation was not eased by the fact that the questionnaire was fairly long and complex. Some children could fill in most of it by themselves, some could not. All the children had to be asked certain questions by the interviewer, and some details, largely administrative were filled in by the interviewer once the interview was completed.

All in all, despite a certain amount of initial misgivings, both children and staff coped extremely well with a task that was time consuming and arduous for both of them!

Most of the questions had pre-printed, pre-coded categories of answers. Five questions were totally open-ended. These five questions were analysed by hand but the remaining twenty-five questions were analysed on a 32K Commodore PET Computer at Central Information Services, Senate House, University of London. One research worker and a temporary assistant spent two rather laborious weeks keying in and retrieving the data. The Commodore was labour intensive but had the advantage of being quite easy to use by staff with no previous knowledge of computers.

2.2 The personal interviews

Researching an age group about which relatively little information is available, it was felt desirable to employ qualitative as well as quantitative methods.
> 'The essence of qualitative research is an unstructured and flexible approach to interviewing that allows the widest possible exploration of views and behaviour'.

A small sub-sample of 20 scheme users was selected to be interviewed on tape. Although the intention was to be informal and flexible, constraints of time meant that a fairly detailed interview schedule was used.

Following a short piloting session, one project worker carried out all the interviews, privately, on library premises. Appointments were made for the children and letters were given to them to take home to their parents.

A dossier was compiled by the researcher on each child, consisting of completed questionnaires, reviews written by the child, comments from librarians and finally, the transcripts of the interviews.

2.3 The samples

2.3.1 Scheme non-users

Scheme non-users were sampled during a full one-week period at each of the eight junior libraries participating in the project.

All library users coming in to the library during this week were asked to complete the first two pages of the questionnaire. No distinction was made, at this stage, between scheme users and non-users. A small proportion of children filling in a questionnaire at this stage decided to join a scheme at a later date and records were amended for these children accordingly.

Of the children completing the questionnaires during this 'saturation' week 168 were scheme non-users. This number does not represent an 'average' count of scheme non-users in any summer week. Scheme non-users tend to drop out of library use during the summer — or become scheme users — and a week in early summer was deliberately chosen in order to achieve a sufficient number of non-users to be able to use them as a control group against scheme users.

Non-response was slight. The library staff were instructed to ensure that no child was distressed by having to fill in a questionnaire, and simply to allow any user who did not want to fill in a questionnaire, not to do so. Despite some initial misgivings concerning children — or parents — who might be worried about filling in a long official-looking form, and about children who might be very flippant in their replies, the response was good (95%) and totally serious.

Composition of the sample of scheme non-users was as follows:

Scheme non-users: sample

Age groups	%	Sex	%
11	23	Boys	42
12	27	Girls	58
13	20		
14	16		
15	9		
16	4		
17	0		
18	(1 person)		

N=168

2.3.2 Scheme users

Scheme users were sampled from the second week up to the end of the schemes. Within this seven week period, the library staff were asked to sample all scheme users, though of course, the size of the final sample achieved had to be less than the total population because interviewing did not start until the second week of Bookmaster. It was known that a proportion of children enrolling in the first week but 'dropping out' almost immediately, would be missed.

In the event, a further proportion of children were 'missed' by the librarians due to the fact that these children dropped out, not immediately, but early on in the scheme, before they had been interviewed. The library staff were allowed to choose at which visit to interview scheme users. It was essential to allow them this manoeuvrability, to enable them to cope with their workloads and it did not affect the representativeness of the sample, except that, as expected, non-completers were under-represented. In fact, the proportion of non-completers in the sample was rather higher than expected.

A total number of 463 children over 11 enrolled in the schemes. The sample numbered 312 with non-completers slightly underestimated, age groups and scheme membership representative, but with girls slightly over-represented. The over-representation of girls in this sample was rectified in the in-depth interview sample, where boys were deliberately over-represented.

Scheme users: sex of total population and sample

	Total scheme population, all age groups %	Sample %	Total population of Bookmasters %
Boys	40	32	34
Girls	60	68	66
	N = 1447	N = 312	N = 201

Scheme users: age groups, total population, and sample

Age groups	Total population %	Sample %
11	36	35
12	33	32
13	18	19
14	8	9
15	2	2.5
16	1	1
17	1	1.5
18	(1 person)	(1 person)
	N = 463	N = 312

Scheme users: total population and sample

	Total population over 11 %	Sample %
Bookmasters	41.5	45
Bookwizards	39	38
Bookworms	19.5	16.5
	N = 463	N = 312

*Scheme users: total population and sample,
proportion completing schemes*

	Total population: all children, all schemes %	Total population of Bookmasters %	Sample %
Completed	60	52	60
Did not complete	40	48	40
	N = 1447	N = 201	N=312

2.3.3 In-depth interviews

Six branch librarians were each asked to select a quota of four children in specific age and sex categories. They were instructed to choose children over a wide ability range.

Appointments were made for these children, all scheme users, to be interviewed on library premises in privacy.

The final sample chosen was as follows:

In-depth interviews: sample

	Age groups							
	11	12	13	14	15	16	17	Total
Boys	3	2	2	—	1	—	1	9
Girls	1	4	3	2	—	1	—	11
Total	4	6	5	2	1	1	1	20
			N = 20					

Each interview lasted between half and three-quarters of an hour.

Appendix 3 Project documents

3.1 Notes for interviewers

BOOKMASTER RESEARCH PROJECT

SUMMER 1981

NOTES FOR INTERVIEWERS

Contents: -

1. Project briefing: Aims, objectives, sources of
                           information.

2. Preparatory work: Pre-testing, piloting, questionnaire
                           design.

3. Interviewing: Selecting respondents, securing
                           cooperation, the interview, avoiding
                           bias, probing versus prompting.

4. Recording responses: Accuracy, completeness, editing,
                           coding.

5. The questionnaire

6. Instructions for piloting

1. PROJECT BRIEFING

Aims

To explore in depth preference of young people aged 11-18, enrolled in Westminster City Childrens Libraries reading schemes, and others in this age group not enrolled in the schemes but using the libraries over the same period of time. (July - September).

To collect basic data on the use, attraction and observable effects of the three reading schemes currently being offered.

To explore certain aspects of library use among young people in this age group.

Research areas of interest

Basic demographic data:	Name, address, age, sex, school, (employment), length of residence, language spoken and read, size of family.
Use of public library:	Branch registered at, junior or adult registration, reason for visit, satisfaction with stock.
Book reading:	Number of books read, sources of books, preferred categories.
Elements of choice:	How/why books are chosen - importance of typeface, layout, format, length, pace, and any other factors.
Use of reading schemes:	Who uses them, how they know about them, why they choose them, preferred aspects, ideas for improvements.
Effects of schemes:	Any observable differences in library behaviour of children taking/taken part in scheme.

Sources of information to be used (excluding piloting work)

a. Survey of scheme users, July 20th to August 29th. Questionnaire administered or supervised by library staff.
b. Sample survey of non-scheme users, July 20th to August 8th. To be carried out over a one-week period in each branch, administered as above.
c. Case studies of selected past scheme users, August. Structured interviews with respondents identified from first phase of interviewing, carried out by researcher.
d. Book chosen by scheme users. Documentary analysis.
e. Reviews written by scheme users. Documentary analysis.
f. Insights from librarians running reading schemes, concerning elements of choice (see above, Research areas of interest). Group discussions.
g. Registration forms for scheme users, completed by all entrants, but only 11-18 group forms to be analysed.

2. PREPARATORY STAGES IN QUESTIONNAIRE CONSTRUCTION

NB: This is the second major stage in the investigation. First stage is delineation of aims and objectives, followed by design of the investigation. Having decided what precisely to do, and having assessed the resources available, you must then decide on the most efficient and reliable method of collecting the information you want. Second major stage of most investigations is preparation of any interview schedules or questionnaires needed.

Pre-testing

This is the early preparatory stage, when questionnaire is being developed. Very often, questions will be added or discarded throughout this stage, also terminology may be altered many times. Any number of pre-tests may be carried out according to necessity and resources available.

Piloting

This is the final preparatory stage, usually in the form of a full dress rehearsal, but on a much smaller scale.

Questionnaire design

Good design is very important. It should ensure an **easy** relaxed interview - easy for the respondent to understand and answer accurately, and easy for the interviewer to administer. Bear in mind the following points:-

- Beware using catchall phrases to save time.
- Beware of long vague questions, or overly complicated pedantic questions.
- Beware of possibly unfamiliar words or phrases - don't pitch it too highbrow or too slangy.
- Avoid sweeping generalisations if possible - its more useful to ask 'Why did you come here today', than 'Why do you usually come here'.
- Avoid double negatives
- Try to avoid hypothetical questions - the answers depend very much on respondents levels of expectations, and some people dislike hypothesising in principle.
- Avoid leading questions - a question that assumes the respondent holds a particular point of view, e.g. 'What is it that you like about your job' is a leading question: 'Do you like or dislike your job', isn't.
- Don't overcrowd the questionnaire - if its difficult to negotiate it will generate faltering questioning and faulty recording.
- Be consistent in layout. Various conventions exist, e.g. all interviewers instructions in upper case, therefore only lower case words should ever be read out by an interviewer.
- Always indicate all instructions to interviewers on the questionnaire, such as whether more than one pre-code may be ringed, etc.
- Give clear filtering instructions. The conventional instruction to indicate moving on to a later question is SKIP TO ...... When filtering is completed, an ASK ALL instruction should be inserted.
- Flow, structure and length of questionnaire should keep respondents interest.
- Ensure adequate space left for verbatim recording of answers.
- Ensure that every question requires an answer.
- Questionnaire construction must allow answers to be edited and coded. All answers have to be given code numbers, the suggested answers are called 'pre-codes'.

PILOTING IS CARRIED OUT TO TEST THE QUESTIONNAIRE FOR ALL
THESE ASPECTS OF DESIGN

3. INTERVIEWING

Selecting respondents

Fortunately, many of the possible problems associated with selecting and securing cooperation of respondents do not apply in this instance. You don't have to go out and find respondents, they are coming to you - literally so in the case of children enrolled in the reading schemes.

Our survey population is the users of eight childrens libraries, aged 11 - 18. For the purpose of this investigation we must exclude any children visiting these libraries when a summer activity is in progress.

a. Children enrolled in reading schemes

All scheme users will register in the usual way on slightly extended forms than you used last year (to ensure that we have some information about the children who drop out). The registration forms will include a few questions to be asked of children who complete their scheme, aged 11 to 18 only.

Apart from the registration form, all scheme entrants, aged 11 to 18, will be required to complete a questionnaire, in the library. You may use your discretion as to when to ask them to do this, but try to err on the early side, to avoid losing any more dropouts than necessary. Complete all interviews by August 29th.

You will find that initial cooperation is fairly easy to secure, but sustaining a neutral tone of interview throughout - establishing a certain amount of 'distance' between you and your 'respondent' will require deliberate effort on your part.

Don't crowd them - give them the choice of completing the questionnaire themselves, be discreet in the help you offer, and the way in which you check their replies.

b. Children not enrolled in reading schemes

This means everyone using your branch, aged 11 to 18, who isn't enrolled in any reading scheme, throughout the week chosen for your branch. Weeks chosen are:-

July 20th to 25th: Paddington, Victoria, Marylebone, Churchill Gardens, Church St, Maida Vale.

July 27th to August 1st: Pimlico

August 3rd to   : Queens Park

You may find initial approach to these children requires some thought - work out your own opening phrases, main thing is to be confident.

Securing cooperation

No one is obliged to complete a questionnaire but you are very unlikely to meet any refusals.

Always emphasise confidentiality and dont breach it.

Be prepared to talk about the purpose of the survey. If you appear to be uninterested or not very serious, your respondent will take his cue from you and behave accordingly.

Be prepared to justify any questions you ask.

If you do meet with any initial refusals, a good ploy is to start asking the questions anyhow. With any luck, natural curiosity and pleasure in having someone listening to their points of view will overcome any initial reluctance.

As the total number of children who are likely to be using your branch in any one week, other than those enrolled in schemes, is not going to be very great (in this age group) it is particularly important to try and achieve 100% coverage.

However, if you do get a refusal, fill in anything you know or have observed about the respondent on a blank questionnaire - even if its just their sex and probable age.

Have all the materials you require to hand and use discretion in allowing respondents privacy. Dont let yourself be interrupted if possible, and dont allow anyone else to look over your shoulder, or your respondents.

As far as possible, treat your respondents as adults - if you imply you are doing this, you will encourage more adult responses. Let them choose whether or not to complete it themselves.

The Interview

You need to reassure your respondent that they are not in an examination, nor an ordinary conversation. They are not being tested but its not just a casual friendly (unimportant) exercise. Therefore, be friendly and relaxed but <u>neutral</u>. Try to keep some distance while being alert to need for help.
Beware of being too helpful by adding frequent words of encouragement - it can imply value judgements on your part.
Your opening phrases will be your own words, but once the interview starts, DONT DEVIATE FROM THE WORDING.
Repeat or read out loud the questions and listed answers if necessary. Try not to answer if they ask you what that means - ask <u>them</u> what they think if means. If they are on the right track anyhow, say so. If not, try to paraphrase only and wait for them to come to some sort of decision. Dont prompt, and dont, on any account, suggest
    possible answers to them, unless they are already listed on the questionnaire.

Avoiding bias

Respondents answers can be distorted by faulty memory, embarassment on sensitive subjects, a tendency to exaggerate or be evasive, or with children, by shyness or difficulty in expressing themselves.
Piloting and good questionnaire design should eliminate much of this, but not necessarily all.
Be careful not to give clues about your own attitudes or expectations or background. Dont reply to questions about what you think (at least not till the interview is completed).
Ask all the questions in a neutral straightforward way and accept the answers in a similar manner. - no surprise, disbelief, oversympathy, slight lowering of the voice, or anything else likely to convey your thoughts on the answer. Consistently maintaining no reaction other than kindly, polite interest is quite difficult in practice, but remember that your role is to help, not just be a friend.
Try to avoid saying 'good' after every reply, it might make the child feel that some answers are more 'correct' than others.
Best way to discourage flippancy or facetiousness is to take the whole exercise seriously yourself.

Probing

Probing is a key interviewing skill. e.g. encouraging the respondent to give an answer. Probing may be verbal - 'Please tell me more about that', - or non-verbal - expectant glances etc.
DONT CONFUSE PROBING WITH PROMPTING. Probing should always be neutral, while prompting involves suggesting an answer.
If you are specifically required by the questionnaire to prompt, your instructions will make this quite clear. If there are no instructions to prompt - dont.
If you notice obvious errors or inconsistencies in replies and query them, be sure that your words and tone of voice, and actions, are neutral.
Be direct and straightforward, with no sign of embarrassment if you do query anything. e.g. 'I notice you have said x. Does that mean(paraphrase answer)".
Dont sound apologetic if you do this.
If you have any reason to doubt validity of a response that respondent maintains is correct, indicate this on a separate piece of paper securely attached to q'aire, signed by you and written in private.

DONT AMEND ANY ANSWERS YOURSELF.

4. RECORDING RESPONSES

Accuracy and completeness

Accuracy and completeness is always important, particularly so in this instance,
as total numbers of non-scheme users isnt very high and 100% completeness is
desirable.
Check every q'aire for completeness and legibility, but you dont need to improve
spelling or grammar.
Dont ever summarize or paraphrase for the respondent - encourage their own use of
language and record verbatim answers.
Follow any instructions on the q'aire implicitly, and indicate by upper case (P) in
brackets whenever you have probed. Dont prompt unless specifically instructed to
do so.
Use blue or black ball point pen and cancel mistakes with an equal sign(=) not a
cross.
Each q'aire has a final section for you to complete - day, date, time, branch,
interviewer. The questionnaires will be collected at frequent intervals and edited
immediately for legibility and completeness, so that if they come back to you for
verification you will remember the interview.

Editing and coding

Editing will start immediately, coding will start as soon as non-scheme users have
all been interviewed.
All answers have to be allocated a code number to allow analysis. Questions that
have a complete list of possible answers attached to them are called 'closed'
questions, and the range of possible answers attached are called 'pre-codes'.
Each pre-code has a corresponding code number.
'Open' questions do not have any pre-codes because the range of answers is not
known in advance . However the answers still have to be coded, which means that
the answers have to be sorted into categories and the categories allocated code
numbers, after the survey has been carried out. This is part of the editing process.
When all editing is complete, coding starts. This is when the information is
transferred, usually onto punch cards for computer analysis.

5. THE QUESTIONNAIRE

The final version of the questionnaire wont be available until piloting finished.
Each branch will receive a batch of blank questionnaires plus notes on use of the
questionnaires.
Ensure that all interviewers:-
a. have read these general notes for interviewers
b. have piloted at least one interview
c. read the notes on use of the questionnaire,
before they start interviewing.

Keep the notes on use of the questionnaire in an accessible place, for reference.
Remember that all completed questionnaires are confidential documents.

6. INSTRUCTIONS FOR PILOTING

1. Anytime between now and closing time this Thursday, pilot the questionnaire on at least one, preferably two, library users aged between 11 and 18. If you do two, try and vary the age group.

2. Piloting is usually carried out on a population similar, but not identical, to your survey population. In other words, you should ideally pilot in a branch not involved in the main survey. If this is impossible, select a respondent at your branch at a quiet time and take them out of the childrens library if possible. You dont want to alert the users of your branch that something is afoot, or give some of them the chance to start thinking of 'good' answers. (Or the chance to avoid ever coming in while the survey is on).

3. Write an assessment of the interview, bearing in mind the following questions:-

   - have you had to repeat or amplify any questions,
   - any difficulties in recording the answers or working through the questionnaire,
   - respondent didnt understand a question or found it ambiguous?
   - did flow of questions seem reasonably natural
   - do pre-codes fit the range of answers given
   - any other unforeseen problems.

4. Attach assessment securely to completed questionnaire. (Make sure you sign them)

5. Have everyones completed questionnaire(s)/assessment ready for collection from your branch on Friday.

GOOD LUCK!

3.2 Questionnaire and registration form

1.

WESTMINSTER YOUNG LIBRARY USERS SURVEY

This survey is being carried out to help to make the library better for you.
You can help us greatly by answering these questions. Please put a tick in
the box next to your answers and leave the other boxes empty. When you have
finished, go back to the librarian. Thank you.

1. How old are you?

11 ☐	15 ☐	1 5	(11)
12 ☐	16 ☐	2 6	
13 ☐	17 ☐	3 7	
14 ☐	18 ☐	4 8	

2. Are you a boy or girl?

boy ☐ girl ☐   1   (12)
2

3. Are you at school or college or work?

(Tick one box only)

school ☐ work ☐   1   (13)
college ☐   2
3
left school, but ☐   4
not yet working

4. How long have you lived in London?

(Tick one box only)

less than 1 year ☐   1   (14)
1-5 yrs ☐   2
over 5 years ☐   3

5. Did you come here today with anyone else?

(You may tick more than one
box if necessary)

friends ☐   1   (15)
parents ☐   2
on my own ☐   3
other people ☐   4
someone else ☐   5

6. Why did you come today?

(You may tick more than one
box if necessary)

to return books ☐   1   (16)
to borrow books ☐   2
to meet friends ☐   3
something to do ☐   4
look something up ☐   5
do homework ☐   6
any other reason?............................
....   7

7. Do you get books to read from
anywhere else, apart from here?
Don't count books you need for
school work.

(You can tick more than one
box if necessary)

parents ☐   1   (17)
school library ☐   2
friends ☐   3
another public library ☐   4
bought yourself ☐   5
other relatives ☐   6

108

P.T.O

8 What kinds of books do you like most of all? YOU CAN
TICK MORE THAN ONE KIND IF YOU WANT BUT NOT MORE THAN FOUR.
Read through the whole list before you make up your mind

historical stories ☐	Science fiction ☐	1 1	(18-19
stories about famous people ☐	animal/pet stories ☐	2 2	
art or craft books ☐	factual books ☐	3 3	
funny stories ☐	magic stories ☐	4 4	
stories you've seen on TV ☐	ghost/horror stories ☐	5 5	
mysteries ☐	war stories ☐	6 6	
adventure stories ☐	love stories ☐	7 7	
stories about teenagers like yourself ☐	sport stories ☐	8 8	
stories about other countries ☐	school stories ☐	9 9	

Others? Please say ....

9 What kind of books would you like us to have more of?
Write your answer here -
(It can be anykind of book, ...
not cnly those listed above)

    ....

    ....

    ....

1 1 (20-
2 2   21)
3 3
4 4
5 5
6 6
7 7
8 8
9 9

IF THIS IS YOUR FIRST VISIT TO THIS LIBRARY PLEASE STOP WRITING NOW, AND

TAKE THIS BACK TO THE LIBRARIAN. If you have been before, please answer
the next two questions before going back to the librarian.

10 Other library users have mentioned problems in finding good books in this
library. Tell us if you agree or disagree with the following things
(You should have five ticks when you have finished).

1. Too many books are too hard to read - I agree ☐   I disagree ☐   1 2 (23)
2. Too many books are too long   - I agree ☐   I disagree ☐   1 2 (24)
3. Too many books are all words (not
   enough drawings)   - I agree ☐   I disagree ☐   1 2 (25)
4. Its difficult to choose a book
   from all the books on the shelves - I agree ☐   I disagree ☐   1 2 (26)
5. I don't understand how all the books
   are arranged   - I agree ☐   I disagree ☐   1 2 (27)

11 And finally, please write down any ideas you have which could make the
library better for you.   ....

    ....

    ....

THANK YOU VERY MUCH FOR YOUR HELP - PLEASE GO BACK TO THE LIBRARIAN NOW

109

3.

CHECK Q's 1 - 11 COMPLETED

12. Are you a Member of Westminster Library?

red token	1	(28)
blue token	2	
not member	3	

IF NOT: Member of any public library?

yes	1	(29)
no	2	

IF YES: Which one? ....

London	1	(30)
not London	2	

13. Are your parents public library members?
(P: ANYWHERE IN COUNTRY) EITHER PARENT

yes	1	(31)
no	2	

14. Are you likely to read any books this summer? [NOT JUST LIBRARY BOOKS]

1 1	
2 2	(32)
3 3	
4 4	

IF YES: How many? (P) .... [IF NONE WRITE NONE]

5 5	(33)
6 6	
7 7	
8 8	

15. How important are the following things in helping you to choose a book?
I am going to read out a list of things other young people have mentioned as
being important to them. Please tell me whether they are important to you or
not. (CIRCLE APPROPRIATE RESPONSE)

	Important	Not important	Don't know/can't answer		
Print not too small?	1	2	3		
Book not too long	1	2	3	1 2 3	(34)
Enough illustrations	1	2	3	1 2 3	(35)
Good picture on front cover	1	2	3	1 2 3	(36)
Good titles	1	2	3	1 2 3	(37)
Reading the blurb	1	2	3	1 2 3	(38)
(EXPLAIN BLURB IF NEC.)			3	1 2 3	(39)
Knowing about the book	1	2			
Seeing the story on TV	1	2	3	1 2 3	(40)
Book seems interesting	1	2	3	1 2 3	(41)
Book not too short	1	2	3	1 2 3	(42)
The writer	1	2	3	1 2 3	(43)
Paperback	1	2	3	1 2 3	(44)
A good story	1	2	3	1 2 3	(45)
Recommendations from other			3	1 2 3	(46)
people	1	2			
and finally, anything else we have forgotten? (P)			3	1 2 3	(47)

....

16. Are you a regular library user? (AT LEAST ONE EVERY 3 WEEKS)

Yes	1	(49)
No	2	

17. What languages do you speak at home? (P) ....
(TRY TO ASCERTAIN PREFERRED LANGUAGE,
FIRST AND SECOND LANGUAGE, AND RECORD) ....

....

1 1 1	
2 2 2	(50)
3 3 3	
4 4 4	(52)
5 5 5	
6 6 6	
7 7 7	
8 8 8	
9 9 9	

18. What languages do you read in? (P) ....
(READING GENERAL FICTION PRIMARILY - IF
CHILD INDICATES READING PREFERENCES DIFFER IN...........................
DIFFERENT LANGUAGES, RECORD)
DON'T INCLUDE LANGUAGES LEARNT AT SCHOOL

1 1	(53)
2 2	
3 3	(55)
4 4	
5 5	
6 6	

19. And finally, what is your address?
(IF YOU CAN CODE DIRECTLY, DO SO, OTHERWISE RECORD
ADDRESS ONLY). (RECORD ADDRESS IN ALL CASES).

West	1	(56)
Inner London	2	
Outer London	3	
Not in London	4	

....
....

THANK RESPONDENT FOR PARTICIPATION AND COMPLETE REST ON YOUR OWN P.T.O

20	Does user belong to a reading scheme?	Yes	1				(57)

| 20 | Does user belong to a | | Yes | 1 | | (57) |

20   Does user belong to a   Yes   1   (57)
     reading scheme?   No   2

21   E.M.G.   1 1 1 (58-
     (REFER TO 2 2 2   60)
     NOTES IF IN   3 3 3
     DOUBT) 4 4 4
                                                      5 5 5
                    .... 6 6 6
                                                      7 7 7
                                                      8 8 8
                                                      9 9 9

     Day ....

     Date ....

     Time interview stated ....

22   Branch ....
                                                A   1   (61-)
                                                G   2
                                                M   3
                                                P   4
                                                Q   5
                                                T   6
                                                V   7
                                                L   8

     Interviewer ....

23   First time library user?   Yes   1   (62)
                                               No   2

SURVEY REGISTRATION FORM: INTERVIEWER COMPLETE Q's 24, 27 ON ENROLMENT
(AGES 11-18 ONLY)

24   What scheme are you enrolled in?

Bookmaster	1	(63)
Book wizard	2	
Bookworm	3	

25   How did you hear about
this scheme?

librarian	1	(64)
parents	2	
school/teachers	3	
friends	4	
advertised	5	
knew it from last year	6	
others:	7	

26   Why did you choose this
scheme and not any others?

....	1	1 (65-
....	2	2 66)
	3	3
....	4	4
	5	5
....	6	6
	7	7
	8	8
	9	9

27   Have you taken part in one
of these reading schemes before?

Yes	1	(67)
No	2	

If yes - which ones [LAST ONE ENTERED ONLY]

bookworm	1	(68)
bookmaster	2	

ALSO - How many times have you
entered a scheme so far

       [ANY SCHEME]

once	1	(69)
twice	2	
3	3	
4	4	
5	5	

COMPLETE LAST THREE QUESTIONS WHEN - AND ONLY IF - SCHEME COMPLETED

P.T.O.

112

- 6

28   What did you particularly like about this scheme?

	liked a lot	quite liked	wasn't important	
having list of books to choose from	1	2	3	(70)
having someone to help me choose the books	1	2	3	(71)
having someone to talk to about the books	1	2	3	(72)
getting a badge	1	2	3	(73)
getting a certificate	1	2	3	(74)
seeing my name up in the library	1	2	3	(75)
going to the presentation ceremony	1	2	3	(76)
seeing my review published	1	2	3	(77)
writing down my ideas about books	1	2	3	(78)
having something to do in the holidays	1	2	3	(79)
any thing else -	1	2	3	(80)

....

29   What did you least like about your scheme?

....

....

....

....

Please write down any ideas you have about what would make the scheme
better for you

30   ....

....

....

....

113

3.3 Notes on the questionnaire

BOOKMASTER RESEARCH PROJECT: NOTES ON THE QUESTIONNAIRE. SUMMER 1981

(These notes are confidential, designed for survey staff only.

General

Record all refusals, with as much information as possible. Cancel mistakes with an equal sign (=) through the square you are cancelling. If any queries arise that aren't covered by these notes, record them on a separate piece of paper, with as much detail as necessary, and contact Erika when you have the time.

All questions except Q.9, Q.11 and Q.21 require an answer.

Name is not asked for on the questionnaires and it is not required for the survey. You may still wish to ask younger children their name, if only to be able to address them by name when you talk to them, and also to discourage the faint possibility of some children filling in another questionnaire with a different interviewer. They are less likely to do this if you know them by name. First name would be quite sufficient, and you could ask for it while guaranteeing confidentiality.

e.g. Before we start, whats your first name? I'm not going to write it down, I just want to know what to call you.

If you think a child has already filled in a questionnaire, let them do it again but ask for their full name this time and write it on the back of the questionnaire.

If for any reason you feel uncomfortable or unable to ask name, dont.

Let respondents fill in first two pages themselves - these notes are for you if queries are brought to you.

Question One

Record age on day of interview.

Question Three

Include all special schools or alternative educational provision as 'school', if child is aged 16 or under.
If person has left school and is doing full-time voluntary work, count as 'work'. (Also Gov. training schemes etc.)
Occasional voluntary work, count as 'not yet working'.
'Not yet working' will include those genuinely between education and work, and those unemployed.

Question Six

Any type of school work, count as 'homework'.

Question Seven

'Books to read' means any recreational reading, as opposed to required reading for education or work.
'School library' mean borrowing or buying from school libraries, but recreational reading only.

Question Eight

Allow 'others' as a fifth category, and use it to record any answers that don't fit into listed categories. If they are close but not identical, record answers under 'others' and editors will recode if necessary.

Question Nine

Don't probe and ignore if unanswered, it isnt necessarily going to be computer analysed.

Question Ten

If this question causes problems, tell responsdents not to think too deeply about it, and rephrase question so that it requires a yes/no answer. e.g. Do you agree that too many books in this library are too hard to read?

Question Eleven

Ditto question nine, see above.

Question Twelve

Name London authorities, name town or city outside London, (or England.) If temporary member, indicate.

Question Thirteen

Either parent, or guardian or adult lived with, will do. Question is designed to elict exposure to library use on the part of a 'significant' adult.

Question Fourteen

This is designed to elict evidence of difference in holiday reading between broad groups of children - we dont set too much store by the accuracy of every individual answer. Probe automatically by translating the answer into books per week.
e.g. If they say 6, say 'that means about 1 a week, does it, as there are six weeks in summer holidays. If their holidays are longer than six weeks, ask them to adjust their answer.

('This summer' means six weeks from mid July to End of August.) Don't restrict reading to library books only, but exclude school work or required reading.

Question Fifteen

This question is important to us, Paraphrase if necessary, as 'Tell me what you look for when you choose a book? Do you look for print thats not too small? Is that important to you or not?

Question Sixteen

Count anyone as a regular user if you know them, and regard them as such in your own mind, even if they rarely borrow books. Otherwise take regular use within three week periods as minimum requirement. Don't include children who only use the library during school holidays, no matter how avid that use might be.

Question Seventeen

Take whatever answers are given, but probe to find 'first' language. This is language preferred at home.

Contd.

Use this question to probe discreetly for ethnic minority group (EMG). (See Q. 21)
In the vast majority of cases the child will tell you how he comes to speak
the languages he says he speaks. Do not upset any child by pursuing this
line of questioning if you are faced with conspicuous silence. If you happen
to know the childs ethnic background anyhow, you dont need to ask any further
questions.

Question Eighteen

This is more important to us than Q. seventeen. We wish to ascertain what
languages the child uses to read recreational materials. Refer back to Q8
if necessary to get at this -
e.g. 'You said you like (love stories) before - what language would you read
those in?
Discount all languages being learnt at full-time day school, for our purposes
we would regard this as school not recreational reading, even though fiction
may be read in such languages.

Question Nineteen

House number isnt necessary, neither is name of flats. We need street and
postal area to analyse catchment areas.

Question Twenty

You can ignore - will be completed by editors at end, if not completed by you.

Question Twenty-One

Dont worry obsessively about this - we arent producing world demographic
statistics! We wish to know whether we are attracting a representative
proportion of local groups of people who may have particular needs or demands.
This is why we collect information on age - different age groups have
different needs and wants. In the same way, ethnic minority groups have
particular needs and/or wants. (We assume we know, and are meeting the needs
of majority ethnic groups). As far as possible, indicate either.
* b. Or known/observable ethnic origin. (Certain third or fourth generation
minority group children - British children - present particular needs and
wants(Chinese and West Indian for example), and we would like to know how
far the library is attracting representative numbers of children in these
groups - and also how representative the libraries clientele is of a highly
multi-cultral area such as Westminster.

Very many people are members of ethnic minority groups, if origin 3 or 4
generations back is taken into account - or are second generation members
of ethnic groups that cannot be identified by appearance or name, or place
of birth. Identification of such individuals is beyond our resources ahd
we can only reasonably hope that such groups do not have any special library
needs.

No response to this question will be taken to mean that you have no evidence
or information that tells you that the child is a member of any minority
ethnic group (minority in this country only of course). If you wish to
indicate that you are only guessing the childs EMG, do so.

Question Twenty-three

Check back to see whether Qs 10 and 11 have been answered to answer this one.

Question Twenty-four - Thirty

Any queries contact Erika

*a. Country of origin of parents (or child) if you have any reason to think it
may be other than Britain.

116

3.4 Interview schedule

DEPTH INTERVIEWS : INTERVIEW SCHEDULE

INTRODUCTION: General questions.......summer holidays....
              family.......live near....

SCHEME USE AND ATTRACTION: Are you enjoying your scheme..
              why....whats the best part.....any bits you dont
              like......did you enjoy as much this year as last.

CHOICE OF FICTION: Is it easy to choose good books....what
              happens at school.....how do you choose books..
              what kind of books do you like.....what about layout/
              blurb/authors.....anything else.....which books of
              these examples would you choose.....prefer fiction or
              non-fiction.....reading during term-time.....

EFFECTS OF SCHEME: Would you have used library as much.....
              read as many books.....same type of books.....
              helped to know libraries/librarians better....
              introduced to new authors.....helped to write
              reviews....do you read other peoples reviews..

CHANGES: Would you like to see anything different about the
              schemes.....non-fiction books....free choice.....
              would you like any changes to library generally...
              do you talk to your librarian....ask for help/advice...
              have you enjoyed the books on your scheme....did
              you have any difficulty choosing good books...what
              was your favourite book.......

3.5 Interview request letter

This matter is being dealt with by:

Extension

My reference   L LHR JM

Your reference

Date

City Librarian
Melvyn Barnes DMA ALA FBIM

Dear ....

Thank you for agreeing to come back on ....
at ....   to talk to us about the books
you like reading.

We hope you have enjoyed being on one of our reading schemes
and look forward to talking to you on ....

Many thanks

Children's Librarian

Other reports

Previous British National Bibliography Research Fund reports are listed below together with the organizations from which they can be obtained.

1   Mann, M. *The reading habits of adults.* 1977. British Library Research and Development Department.
2   Bell, L J. *The large print book and its user.* 1980. Library Association.
3   Bell, L J. *A close circuit television project for the visually handicapped.* 1979. British Library Lending Division.
4   Cooke, M. *Public library provision for ethnic minorities in the UK.* 1979. Leicestershire Library Services.
5   Verma, G K. *Feasibility study of books and ethnic minorities.* 1981. British Library Lending Division.
6   Ingham, J. *Books and reading development.* 1981. Bookshops.
7   Curwen, A G. *The use of ISBNs compared with keywords as means of retrieving bibliographic records on-line.* 1981. British Library Lending Division.
8   Gagan, C. *A Sample and analysis of publications appearing in the British National Bibliography not carrying Standard Book Numbers.* 1980. British Library Lending Division.